Spirit OF Love

My attention was drawn toward the middle of the theater, where I could see a beautiful baby boy being held above a woman's head. The baby was floating like an angel. I pointed to a young woman several rows from the stage. Understandably, she was too upset to speak, so I asked her if she would come up and see me when the meeting had concluded. The spirit world wished to give her love and reassurance that her baby was safe and happy.

After feeling the woman's sadness, I smiled to myself when the next message came through from spirit. It was from an elderly gentleman named Edward, who asked me to wait, and wait I did, as he walked ever so slowly toward me to continue his communication. While I waited, I found his daughter in the audience. She was laughing so hard, and said this was typical of her father when he was alive—he would just walk in a slow shuffle and everyone had to wait for him.

About the Author

Jenny Crawford has been a teacher, lecturer, and international medium for the past twenty-five years. She is the author/narrator of several meditation tapes, conducts spiritual development workshops, seminars, and lectures, and gives both public and private clairvoyant demonstrations and readings.

Living half the year in New Zealand and the other half of the year in the United States, the author maintains a satellite office in Southern California. She became an ordained minister in 1999.

To Write to the Author

If you wish to contact the author or would like more information about this book, please write to the author in care of Llewellyn Worldwide and we will forward your request. Both the author and publisher appreciate hearing from you and learning of your enjoyment of this book and how it has helped you. Llewellyn Worldwide cannot guarantee that every letter written to the author can be answered, but all will be forwarded. Write to:

Jenny Crawford
℅ Llewellyn Worldwide
P.O. Box 64383, Dept. 0-7387-0273-0
St. Paul, MN 55164-0383, U.S.A.

Please enclose a self-addressed stamped envelope for reply, or $1.00 to cover costs. If outside U.S.A., enclose international postal reply coupon.

Many of Llewellyn's authors have websites with additional information and resources. For more information, please visit our website at http://www.llewellyn.com.

JENNY CRAWFORD

SPIRIT

OF
Love

A MEDIUM'S MESSAGE
OF LIFE BEYOND DEATH

2002
Llewellyn Publications
St. Paul, Minnesota 55164-0383, U.S.A.

FIRST EDITION
First Printing, 2002

Book interior design and editing by Connie Hill
Cover design by Kevin R. Brown
Cover image © 2002 by Photodisc

Library of Congress Cataloging-in-Publication Data
Crawford, Jennifer Christine, 1955–
    Spirit of love : a medium's message of life beyond death / Jenny Crawford. — 1st ed.
        p.   cm.
    Includes bibliographical references.
    ISBN 0-7387-0273-0
    1. Future life. 2. Spiritualism. I. Title.

BL535.C73   2002
133.9—dc21   2002030060

Llewellyn Worldwide does not participate in, endorse, or have any authority or responsibility concerning private business transactions between our authors and the public.

All mail addressed to the author is forwarded but the publisher cannot, unless specifically instructed by the author, give out an address or phone number.

Any Internet references contained in this work are current at publication time, but the publisher cannot guarantee that a specific location will continue to be maintained. Please refer to the publisher's website for links to authors' websites and other sources.

Llewellyn Publications
A Division of Llewellyn Worldwide, Ltd.
P.O. Box 64383, Dept. 0-7387-0273-0
St. Paul, MN 55164-0383, U.S.A.
www.llewellyn.com

Printed in the United States of America

Dedication

I dedicate this book to God. I thank God for blessing me with the opportunity of meeting so many wonderful people—you are all members of my spiritual family.

To my mother Anneliese, for her unconditional love, memories engraved in my heart forever.

To Elma Farmer, a great medium, my mentor and spiritual teacher. Thank you for your wisdom and golden light, which still shines brightly from above.

Table of Contents

Acknowledgments

To all the people who had the courage to share their true life stories; without you this book would not have been possible.

To Corinn Codye, Stephanie, and Professor Hans Holzer for suggesting I contact Llewellyn Worldwide.

To Cassandra Anneliese for bringing such a bright light of joy into our hearts.

To Cassie's mom Sharlene, my soul sister, friend, and medium.

To Donna at Peaceful Living Publications, for all your help.

To Richard Webster, for your insight, wisdom, and encouragement.

To all our loving friends in the United States and throughout the world who have opened their hearts and homes, allowing us to be part of their families.

To all my family, I love you; and lastly to my beloved husband Robert, always the wind beneath my wings . . .

My love and gratitude to you all.

Foreword

by Richard Webster

There has been a strange lack of good books that clearly explain what mediums are, and what they do. I am delighted that Jenny Crawford has written *Spirit of Love*, as it answers all the questions people are likely to ask about the mediumistic world. It also shows the valuable role mediums play in our society.

I can think of no one better than Jenny to write this book. I have followed her career with great interest, and know many people who have benefited from her work. Her mentor, Elma Farmer, was a highly gifted medium who dedicated herself to nurturing and encouraging people who showed promise in the psychic world. Elma was aware of Jenny's remarkable talents from the very start, and must be very pleased that Jenny has developed the international reputation she enjoys today.

Jenny's rise to her current position as one of the world's leading mediums has not been easy. Like everyone in her field, she has experienced opposition and setbacks, and many lesser people would have given up. Fortunately, Jenny continued on her chosen path. We can all learn from her experience and insights.

Spirit of Love is full of personal stories that show how much Jenny's work helps others. The countless letters she has received from others add further testimony to this. These stories also tell us much about Jenny, and her love and concern for humanity.

I found the whole book fascinating, but was particularly interested in the chapter on suicide. I have spent a great deal of time counseling people who have attempted suicide, and have also helped people come to terms with the tragic deaths of family members who killed themselves. Jenny first wrote about this in *Through the Eyes of Spirit*, but provides much more insight and helpful advice in this book, demonstrating how she is continuing to grow and develop. This chapter alone offers enormous comfort to relatives and friends who have been left behind.

The chapter of questions and answers ("What Does It Mean, Jenny?") is a particularly useful one that covers all the questions people are likely to ask about mediums.

However, it is difficult to pick out just one or two chapters in a book such as this, as Jenny's warmth, enthusiasm, and compassion are visible on every page. This is the perfect book for people who want to know more about the spirit world, and Jenny is an excellent teacher.

Introduction

There are Infinite ways to discover your true
Being, but love holds the brightest torch. If
you follow it, you will be guided beyond the
limits of age and death. Come out of the circle
of time and find yourself in the circle of love.

Ageless Body, Timeless Mind
—Deepak Chopra

My first book, *Through the Eyes of Spirit,* was published in 1996, and the response has been overwhelming. I have received thousands of letters, emails, and phone calls from the United States, Canada, South Africa, England, New Zealand, and Australia; many from people in need. I have tried to respond to people personally, and I apologize to those people whom I have missed. I trust that after reading my second book many of your questions will be answered.

I was guided to write my first book to introduce myself and to let people know what it is like to work as a spiritual medium by sharing information on my psychic abilities. I feel very blessed to have been chosen as a medium and to be able to personally write about true-life experiences.

This book is designed to help heal and touch the hearts of many bereaved people. So many people are now open to the subject of life after death; because an unsurmountable level of proof has been put forward, skeptics are struggling to disprove the genuine messages given by spiritual mediums.

Over the years I have had the privilege of seeing thousands of people for private readings, which I will talk about later in the book. These people come from all walks of life: doctors, nurses, therapists, psychologists, hairdressers, social workers, carpenters, mechanics, actors; the list goes on. On average, 70 percent of these people come to seek a connection with a loved one who has passed over into the spirit world. Others come to gain guidance, direction, inner peace, and confirmation of their life's purpose.

I find my work as a medium comes with a requirement for the utmost responsibility and integrity. Confidentiality is a must, and I am always aware of people's sensitivity and feelings. The spirit world seems to deliver messages to each individual differently, and this depends on the person's sensitivity and needs. It is always interesting to hear a message from spirit delivered softly or in a sharp and firm manner; the spirit world seems to decide what is best for the client and how they will receive the message.

One of the stories I share in this book is a strong indicator of how hard a spirit works to communicate with a close friend or loved one on the earth plane. This story is about the famous singer Karen Carpenter and how she appeared to me in a reading, giving profound messages to my client, who had been her sound engineer and tour manager.

I also have chosen some of the most heart-wrenching letters and stories to share with you. For example, a man named Jack lost his only son as a result of an automobile accident. The pain of this tragedy was more difficult for him to bear than the years he spent serving in Vietnam and as a policeman.

Jack was visibly shaken and stunned when I was able to tell him his son had manifested himself to me while waiting for his father to walk through the door. Jack was in shock for quite some time as proof of life after death was revealed to him.

When I see a spirit this way it is called clairvoyance.

How I Became a Medium

So many people ask me how I got started and how a medium works, and what happens when we pass through the veil, which has been described as the temple of beyond. Some also may say it represents the mystical state of "after-death." The veil is the curtain between us and the spirit world—it is this transparent curtain that we must pass through to reach the spirit world. I will talk more in depth about this subject in the book. It can be a helpful tool of preparation and understanding for those suffering a terminal illness or who are present at a loved one's passing.

But the spirit world isn't all about loss and suffering. Many people have shared magical true-life stories that have been orchestrated by the spirit world, and I recount one in particular that occurred while we were on tour in California in 1996. Titled "Mother's Day," it will touch many hearts.

I do believe it is the love link that helps a spirit make a clear communication with a loved one. Unfortunately, I am not able to dial a number and call up a spirit; think of how rewarding this would be if we were able to do so. We could give Elvis Presley a call and also ask to speak to our beloved Princess Di. It is the spirit, however, who connects through me in a reading to speak with their love link on earth.

I have felt guided to write again about the subject of suicide, which sadly affects so many of our young ones. This book is designed to touch and help to heal those broken hearts who may feel they have lost their purpose to move forward in life.

Throughout this book I have tried to share many genuine experiences with you. I believe that God blessed me with a very special gift as a bridge between this world and the spirit world, and that it is my duty to bring you proof of life beyond death. I welcome you to journey with me, as we share the vital links and wisdom that enable each of us to be guided to open our hearts and minds, so that we can receive vital healing, inner peace, and strength as our everyday lives are constantly engulfed by the spirit of love.

I believe that I inherited some of my psychic gifts from my mother's father. My Jewish grandfather, born in Germany, was very psychic. Prior to the outbreak of World War II he had strong premonitions about the tragic events that were in store for the Jewish people. He tried to discuss his psychic visions with other family members, warning them that if they did not flee Germany, it would cost them their lives.

Not all of them listened to him, and most of them were killed in concentration camps, with the exception of one aunt and uncle who committed suicide by tying their legs together and jumping off a bridge.

My grandfather knew it was time to leave Germany when a Gestapo car was parked outside their home. My mother was ten years of age at the time, and my grandfather told her that they were taking a holiday—she had no idea that they would not be returning to their home. They left the house with just a few personal possessions, leaving behind the entire house-lot, as though they were out for a family picnic. They managed to escape Germany along with a few family members. My grandfather's psychic gift saved their lives. After being in hiding for more than two years, they eventually ended up living in Wellington, New Zealand.

We all inherit a certain amount of our psychic awareness. As a young child I always felt a strong and loving presence walking beside me on a pathway filled with light.

I feel I was guided by the spirit world, at the age of eighteen, to join a development circle. This weekly circle was run by Elma Farmer, a well-known New Zealand medium. This is where I began to understand and develop my psychic and spiritual gifts. Elma was strong on discipline, and we were taught that our circle time was precious. She made it very clear that she would not tolerate any of the group engaging in idle chatter during our tuning-in time. During the circle we had to concentrate and pay attention, as we learned how to meditate, administer healing, practice psychometry, and tune in to give one another psychic messages. After the session we would sit and have a cup of tea, and catch up on each other's news.

In this group I was taught how to link with my spiritual guides and teachers. A spirit guide is an evolved soul who resides in the spirit world, who is assigned to work with an individual, teaching and guiding them along their pathway of life. In a religious sense, a spirit guide can also be termed a guardian angel. I have six spiritual guides working with me from time to time, and it has taken me many years to identify my spirit guides. My guides and teachers work with me on various occasions. For example, we each have one main guide. Your main spiritual guide is with you from the moment you take your first breath in life, and departs with you as you take your last breath and leave the earth plane. My main guide is Amos, who is Greek. He brings forth love and compassion and consoles those who are grieving. Amos helps me to make the connection between my client and those who have passed over into the spirit world. Amos works with the vibration of my client and the spirit, enabling me to raise my level of consciousness to make the vital link between both parties. This is where clairvoyance comes in, and I am often able to see the spirit that is communicating. When I hear the spirit talking to me, sometimes with an accent, this is called clairaudience.

I have a Chinese guide who works with me in bringing forth wisdom. My Native American Indian guide works with health and brings forth healing. I have a gentleman working with me who wears a gray suit—he is my business guide. I also have a lady from India who brings with her a very happy and cheerful vibration and shares positive guidance in people's personal lives, and lastly a Tibetan monk who brings peace and tranquility with him.

I can feel a subtle change in my face when one of my guides is with me. Some people experience a tingling at the back of their head, neck, or a tight band around their face. Sometimes when a guide is present your eye will begin to water and a tear appears. Our guides use many different methods to gain our attention.

Overall, our guides bring forth tremendous love and wisdom, and your connection with your spirit guides should fill every cell of your entire being with this love. It does take a long time to recognize your spiritual guides, so be patient. We also have teachers and helpers assigned to us from the spirit world, who are evolved souls. One of your spirit guides acts as your doorkeeper; this is the guide who tries to protect you through life. The doorkeeper works with you subconsciously advising you how to take the correct turns along your pathway of life, and of course we all have free will to go wherever we desire.

Your other guides can change over a period of time, and as we move forward in life, we are assigned different guides to assist with our level of progression. For instance, sometimes you may feel a change within yourself, and this is because a new spirit guide is coming into work with you, teaching you aspects of life that you have not encountered before. Through the art of meditation you will learn how to connect with your spirit guide. You may find my meditation "Meeting up with your Guardian Angels" at the end of the book very helpful. This meditation is also designed to help you connect with your spirit guides.

Being a medium means that people allow you into the privacy of their lives, and this does make me feel truly humble. As a bridge between this world and the spirit world, I feel very privileged to continue to work toward expanding my spiritual and psychic gifts. I urge you to work hard with your development and expansion, and remember that we all have the ability to hear and see spirit.

1

Soul Rescue Work

I choose to believe that each one of us has an
individual soul, that there is One Spirit, the
Spirit of God, going through each and every
one, and that makes each and every one of us
akin, that makes all life and nature akin; for
life in every form is dependent upon that
force we call God.

The Lost Memoirs of Edgar Cayce
—A. Robert Smith

*D*o you ever have that feeling that you are
not alone? Even when the house is empty?
Sometimes, when a person dies, their ego holds
them to the physical body. Other times the person
who has died does not realize that his or her life on
earth has ended. The person may have never considered that there is life beyond death. (The film *The
Sixth Sense* with Bruce Willis is in my view a very
descriptive portrayal of what happens when a person
passes over and does not realize that his physical
body has died.)

Encounters with these spirits are not always gruesome or frightening, as I discovered in 1999 when I had an exciting experience while staying in a beautiful, angelic home in San Marcos, California. For about two weeks I had felt a strong presence in the house. I really didn't take much notice, as I do feel spirit around me most of the time. My husband Rob and I were planning a holiday with our dear friends, Lars and Gloria, and so I ignored the spirit presence as the four of us went off for a two-week vacation together.

Upon our return home, Lars and Gloria's daughter, Britta, had felt a presence in the house. Britta is a paramedic, an earth angel, and is very intuitive. She told us that one day she came down the stairs in the house and some of the kitchen cupboards were open.

On another occasion she was showering and heard a man's voice call out "hello." She replied back to him, thinking it was her brother visiting the house, but when she came out of the shower the house was empty, or at least no one was visibly present.

Another time she was driving her car to work, and had such an overwhelming feeling of a man in the backseat that she stopped in the street to investigate. Her vehicle was empty, even though the hairs on the back of her neck and arms were still standing up strongly.

After hearing Britta's report, I felt there was a spirit in the house. I had a strong urge to investigate the upstairs bathroom, and I can almost always guarantee that a spirit is in a particular room when I feel this way.

They also seem to like being in bathrooms; it may be the water flow that gives them energy.

That night when I was drifting off to sleep I was awakened by footsteps in the bedroom. I said the Lord's Prayer and fell back to sleep. I went into a deep, deep slumber and then I was aware of a man lying behind me in the bed; even though I felt the presence, I could not open my eyes. I did not feel afraid at anytime as he stretched his large hands around my body and held my hands tightly with both of his. I could see a vision of a tall, well-dressed man in a suit wearing black, polished shoes. As he continued to hold my hands very tightly, I began to pray and pray. I reached for his hands and placed them in the air pointing toward the sky. I asked him to go to God and to be beamed up to the light. As I continued to say the Lord's Prayer I saw him start to lift up. I prayed four times and each time I could see his arms and hands raised up in the air facing toward the light. His feet started to float off the ground and he looked as though he was floating through a field of white clouds.

I believe he had come to me because he knew I could help to rescue his soul. I felt he had been in a motor accident, and had followed paramedic Britta home.

This man had come to me to be released. He was afraid to let go for fear of the unknown. He waited for me to return to the house, as he was guided to me to help release his soul and send him toward the light.

Through the power of prayer he was sent home to the spirit world, and his soul was released and rescued. I felt a peace come over me as he moved toward heaven, and the house settled down again very quickly. Even though he was a stranger to me, I felt privileged to have helped him to free his spirit, and the feeling I got while seeing him rise up to the light will stay with me forever.

I cannot tell you how humbled and wonderful I felt to be a part of this man's transition, as some souls do have great difficulty passing through the veil. They may have passed over very quickly or in an unbearable situation—for example, in tragic circumstances, they could have been murdered, or died in a prison. The conditions surrounding a person's death do determine the level of peace they take with them into the next life. I have had communication with many spirits who have not realized that they are now in another dimension. The spirit may think that they are still living on the earth plane. They are called earthbound spirits or lost souls. These souls feel they have not completed their life's work or lessons on earth, and choose to stay in spirit form as they hover around familiar surroundings and still-living love links.

Some spiritual groups gather together on a regular basis to help these souls pass through the veil. The group sits together in a circle, praying that they will receive love and light. During these circles a telepathic communication is made through a medium, or a member of the spiritual group, to help send the earthbound soul on their way. This helps to release the soul from this earthly world, and allows them to be free spirits, enabling their earthbound soul to transcend to the spiritual realms as they float upward through the transparent curtain of the veil.

2

Being Helped
Through the Veil

As an old Tibetan proverb puts it, "The next
life or tomorrow—we can never be certain
which will come first."
Ethics for the New Millennium
—His Holiness, the Dalai Lama

*D*uring a reading it is always pleasing to hear
from a spirit that loved ones were present at
the time of their passing. Even holding the hand of a
loved one nearing the time of passing can contribute
to a more comfortable and peaceful transition. The
reassurance and understanding given by family and
friends to those about to pass over will enable them
to travel out of their physical bodies toward an illuminating light. The light shines strongly, allowing
the soul to be guided through the veil.

The veil has been described as the temple of
beyond, or some may say it represents the mystical
state of afterdeath. The veil is the curtain between

the spirit world and us, and it is this transparent curtain that we all must pass through to reach the spirit world.

It is also common for a person close to passing to have an out-of-body experience, in which they visit family and friends. During this time of transition, the visitation occurs while the family member or friend is in their sleep state. The person about to pass over is able to travel on the astral level, out of their physical body, enabling them to connect with the dreams or subconscious state of another. In astral traveling, a person leaves the physical body and can show him or herself to another person by manifesting in a spiritual way, yet still appearing to another person in the physical form.

I believe it is a blessing to be able to say goodbye to loved ones before they leave, as many people do not have the privilege of farewelling a loved one into the spirit world. In our daily lives we may say goodbye to a relative or friend, and shortly afterward hear the shocking news that they have been killed in an accident. It is important to tell our family and friends every day that we love them, even if they are just visiting the corner store. Hugs and messages of love on a daily basis play such an intricate part in our lives. Always leave loved ones with kind and loving words, for this may be the last time you see them.

I recall reading for an eighteen-year-old girl who had a quarrel one afternoon with her younger brother, aged fifteen. She told him, "I wish you were dead."

These were the last words she said to her brother. At 5.30 P.M. that day the family received the tragic news that he had been killed in a car accident. I believe the spirit world was instrumental during our session together in helping to console her grief and ease the guilt that she had carried with her since her brother's passing.

A guardian angel is an evolved soul who is assigned to guide and watch over each of us from the time of our birth. In many instances this guardian angel from the spirit world comes to the aid of a soul to guide them through the veil and into their next life. The guardian angel appears in ethereal form and guides the soul through the tunnel of light and into the spiritual realms where healing and learning continue to take place.

The guardian angel brings along an energy that appears as a bright illuminating light, guiding the soul through its transition to the spirit world. This light beams off the silver cord that connects the soul to the physical bodies. When the Silver cord is severed, the physical body is no longer able to function without a soul, leaving behind an empty shell. People who are privileged to be present at the time of a person's passing will often report seeing a shining light fill the room. This occurs when the silver cord is severed and transition to the spirit world takes place.

Some people may experience complete darkness for a period of time after leaving their physical body, then gradually see the light beaming toward them.

When a person is close to death and at their lowest ebb, they can resist leaving because they are concerned about family or feeling they have unfinished business to resolve. These feelings of sadness and confusion can make it more difficult for the soul to leave. In situations like this the person about to pass often sees an apparition of a loved one who has already passed over. The spirit comes forth to communicate with them and to take them by the hand into the next life.

The spirit manifests as an apparition by visualizing a picture of how they appeared when living on the earth plane. The power of this thought projects a transmitted image of the soul that the dying person recognizes, enabling them to see a clear vision of how their loved one looked while living in the physical form. For instance, they could show themselves wearing denim jeans and a blue shirt if that was the familiar type of clothing they wore when they were alive.

I was called to our local hospital to give spiritual support to a woman named Janet whose husband, Jeff, was dying of motor neuron disease. This disease shuts down the nerves and muscles in the body, and causes total paralysis. Jeff was in his early forties, and had been ill for approximately a year.

Jeff's entire body was paralyzed from the disease, except for one of his big toes. Miraculously he wrote a book about his experiences on a text typewriter before he passed. One profound comment that Jeff wrote just days before he passed over was: "I have been to death's

door and back again. Your life does not flash
you quickly, it moves past you very slowly."

I had been to their home the previous w— —
Janet a reading. During our session, Jeff's brother John,
who had passed over several years ago, came through in
the reading. He asked Janet to pass on the message that
he was waiting for Jeff, and to tell his brother not to be
afraid of dying. It was interesting to see Jeff looking
over my left shoulder when I was in his hospital room.
I am sure he could see his brother John standing in the
room, as the spirit world had begun preparations to
take Jeff through the veil. It was his wish to not die in
the hospital, and he passed over peacefully at his home
three days later.

Jeff was a very spiritual individual and had a strong
understanding of the afterlife. Each individual who
crosses over into the next life does so according to their
beliefs, feelings, and the conditions they created for
themselves while living on the earth plane. We create our
own heaven and our own hell through our conscious
minds; we reap what we sow in each lifetime. We are all
given free will and it is this freedom that determines
which pathway we choose to walk in life, whether it is
good or bad. Buddhists and Hindus believe that an individual's karma is determined upon a person's actions in
one incarnation, creating his or her fate in the next life.
Every thought and action manifested in each lifetime
contributes toward our destiny and level of existence in
the next life. How a person finishes their journey in this

life can affect how they start their next incarnation, or new life.

Reincarnation is a rebirth of one's soul in a different bodily form. When a person passes over to the spirit world, the soul makes its entrance back again into the physical human form as a new baby.

It is always with great sadness in the spirit world when a soul reincarnates back to the earth plane. I have heard my spiritual guides say that the spirit world grieves as the soul is reborn or comes back to earth. The sadness stems from other spirits who have bonded spiritually and shared the light with this special soul.

The opposite applies when a soul returns to the spirit world and the guardian angels rejoice to have them back in heaven again. This is why some people organize their loved one's funeral service as a celebration, rather than a time of mourning. They generally have a spiritual understanding and know that the soul has passed into the realms of happiness, peace, and tranquility. Many people make their own funeral service arrangements prior to passing and they often request the service to be conducted in a celebratory manner.

In the spirit world special healing bays are prepared for each individual who passes through the veil, where they go to recover from their life's experiences and the process of transition. The healing bays are an area where they are taken to according to the conditions of their passing. The healing bay is designed as a place for the soul to enlighten their conscious awareness and understanding of the physical or emotional pain that was endured while living.

In some instances, before a person passes over to the spirit world they try to distance themselves emotionally from those they love. This lightens the burden for the soul to leave their earthly life by temporarily disconnecting their affections from the very people they love. Family and friends should not be disheartened by their loved one's emotional detachment, as this can be a normal occurrence before a soul passes through the veil. Take comfort in knowing that, as they near the time of their passing, they are distracted by spiritual activity around them as those in the spirit world prepare for their homecoming. The person leaving is already in an altered state of consciousness and feeling the presence of spirit around them. They must concentrate to gain the vital energy required to make their journey into the spiritual realms, where understanding of your love connection will be strengthened once again.

In times when a person's passing is drawing closer it can be very helpful to talk softly to them. Hold their hand and explain to them that they have nothing to fear. Many people are afraid to let go because they fear the unknown. They do not know whom they will meet up with or where they are going. Some dying people may feel very weak and vulnerable at this critical time. The comforting presence of a loved one can be instrumental in preserving their dignity and promoting calm expectation of a peaceful passing.

Some people have difficulty communicating before they pass over, particularly those suffering from Alzheimer's disease. They do not always realize where they are going. Alzheimer's patients respond beautifully to the memories of music, and it is a good idea to play their favorite music to soothe them before they depart the earth plane. This can be very helpful as they near the time to leave their physical body behind.

As the time gets closer to your loved one's passing, reassure them confidently that they are loved and well protected for their magnificent journey ahead.

You may choose to tell them you wish to take them with you into a beautiful garden. Let them imagine the sights and smells as you describe any tranquil garden of your choice. Once you feel they have linked with you in this magnificent place of beauty and the time is right, tell them they can now see a stile (a set of steps attached to and crossing over a fence). Ask them to step up onto this stile, an easy step up, and explain to them that you are unable to come with them any further. Tell them you love them and give them permission to cross the fence and go on without you. By giving your loved one permission to leave the earth plane and cross over the stile, you are enabling them to let go of their earthly existence.

Give them reassurance that their angel will be coming to meet them at the stile to help them into the light of the spiritual realms. Reassure them that in God's timing you will see one another again and be linked together in the spirit world. I believe that close love links continue on into several different lifetimes together.

You may also wish to discuss a prearranged sign or password they can use when the time comes for them to communicate with you from the spirit world.

I remember seeing a woman named Sandra who asked for a sign from her son in the spirit world. Prior to our meeting, Sandra spoke to her son in her mind, telling him that in order for her to believe and verify it was genuinely him, he would need to show her lots of apples in the reading. It was a relief for Sandra when I was shown an abundance of apples and apple trees. I was interested to hear that her son had worked on an apple orchard before his death. Even though the message was simple, it was effective for Sandra, and the apples showed her that her son was indeed alive and well in the spiritual realms.

Our loved ones hear our silent thoughts and prayers, they draw in close to our love connection and when a spirit wishes to make contact with us they will always find a way.

Of course, it is important to pray for the living as well as those who have passed on, and the power of prayer can be directed and received many miles away from the point of origin.

I have met people who will not give their loved ones permission to leave the earth plane. This happened to a woman named Cathy, whose spouse passed over with cancer.

She had refused to tell him he had permission to leave the earth plane, and this became evident during the reading. Her spouse was earthbound and needed help to lift his soul to the spirit world. By giving him permission to complete his transition, she would have been telling him it was okay to leave. After Cathy's husband died, it was exhausting for her as he continued to walk beside her in spirit form, latching onto her energy field because he felt she still needed him. One of my jobs as a medium is to help elevate these souls up to the light.

During our reading, I could feel her husband's energy levels rise within a few moments, as he made a safe transition toward the light. I knew Cathy also would start to feel emotionally uplifted and more energetic within a few weeks, as her spouse continued his journey in peace to the higher realms.

On another occasion I met with a woman named Betty whose spouse also was walking beside her in spirit form. I saw a clear vision of him as he walked into the room. He had passed over from a brain tumor, which created confusion for him at the time of his death. Betty knew he was walking beside her, and was not sure how to help him on his way. During our time together in the reading, and through the power of prayer, he followed the light to the other side.

In most cases, the power of love and prayer will direct a person to be with a loved one in their time of need prior to their passing.

I recall meeting Maureen, a woman who was in her early forties, and spoke with a broad Scottish accent. As I started Maureen's session, it was only a few moments before I heard a woman in the spirit world identify herself as May.

"I am Maureen's grandmother on her mother's side," May told me.

Maureen looked surprised as I conveyed this message to her. "My grandmother passed over only a week ago," she told me.

May went on to tell me that Maureen had been with her, and had held her hand when she died.

"Please thank my darling Maureen for praying and helping me; she is just what I needed at the time," the grandmother told me.

With this message, Maureen let out a shriek in Gallic and told me that her grandmother had said exactly the same thing to her, word for word, moments before she passed over.

Many different cultures identify with their own level of understanding and protocol when it comes to bereavement, and this helps them to accept and aid their loved one's passing.

I remember reading for a Hawaiian mother who had lost her thirty-four-year-old son. He was killed as a result of an accident while riding a skateboard in front of his family, and his baby son had died tragically twelve months prior to his own accidental death. I remember his mom saying to me, "We understand where our son is. We look at it like this; he won the race."

Her explanation came with great understanding, as she felt he got to the spirit world before the remaining family members. She also found comfort in the healing thought that he was called to be with his son in the spirit world.

She went on to say, "I used to tell my son how afraid I was of seeing a person after they had died. He always used to say, 'Mom, it's not the dead you should be afraid of, it's the living.'"

Death teaches us so much about suffering, forgiveness, compassion, unconditional love, unfinished business, and finding peace. It also reiterates the message of how precious every waking moment is to each of us, and, most importantly, how it enhances our awareness of God, teaching us to count our blessings and search for the goodness within each individual.

In many instances, before an individual passes through the veil, they may sit upright in bed and start smiling or mention a person's name who has already passed over. Dying people have many different mannerisms and ways of communicating, other than words. It is sometimes as though a reunion is taking place around the deathbed.

One of our dearest friends, Rhoda, told me that when her sister Gayle was dying of cancer, she asked Gayle, "Who is looking at you now through the window?"

Gayle replied, "All of them are."

Rhoda asked, "Are you afraid of them?"

Gayle replied, "Yes, I am not ready to let go yet."

That is why it is important to talk a patient through their time of passing to a safe place where they can float and feel as free as an albatross in flight. Ask them about the special moments of their life, and who they were happiest with, then encourage them to remember those people and time periods. Tell them there is no need to answer you, as often, if they can hear you, you can see the answer in their eyes.

Again, reassure them they are moving to a lovely place where they will feel safe, and ask them to go on from there. Many people find that a loved one who has passed on will come to visit them in the sleep or meditative state to reassure them of their safe passage to the spirit world.

In Rhoda's situation, Gayle came to her in a meditation and said, "Don't be afraid when it is your time to go, I'll be with you." She then placed Rhoda's hand on a warm soft white sheet that felt like a cloud with a silver lining. "See how lovely it is here," she said.

From that moment onward, Rhoda told me, she felt that when her time comes to leave her earthly existence, she will have no fear.

Some people are not afraid to die, which makes their transition so much easier. It is as though they are wrapped up in a cocoon of protection, always feeling safe through life and knowing there is no need to be afraid. Many souls will report that they are very happy in the spirit world and their passing was like taking a magic carpet ride.

I believe that before an individual passes over, they choose the time, location, who is going to be present with them for their last moment in this lifetime on earth, or whether they wish to be alone.

Dying people may also try to wait for an important occasion or date to pass over on, like a birthday, anniversary, or perhaps a holiday.

The dying leave us with so many memories and wonderful gifts, teaching us to be good listeners and enhancing our intuition as we look for vital signs to satisfy them, bringing forth love and peace in their final minutes in this lifetime.

Embracing and comforting just one soul in life as they pass through the veil is truly a magnificent gift to behold. It is exciting to imagine that this is the beginning of a magical life for your loved one. Be patient, for when the time is right, you could be blessed to have a visitation from this special person in your dream state.

3

Karen Carpenter's Story

I embrace my inner child with Love. I take
care of my inner child. It is the child who is
frightened.

It is the child who is hurting. It is the child
who does not know what to do. I will be there
for my child. I embrace it and Love it and do
what I can to take care of its needs. I make
sure to let my inner child know that no
matter what happens, I will always be there
for it. I will never turn away or run away. I
will always love this child.

Letters to Louise
—Louise L. Hay

I met Michael and Debbie Lansing in Southern
California when I was asked to give them both
readings on separate occasions. I was immediately
struck by how genuine and kind this couple was.
While reading for Michael I discovered that he had
been the sound engineer and tour manager for the
famous singers Richard Carpenter and his sister, the
late Karen Carpenter.

A few weeks after reading for Michael, he posted me
a letter and asked if I would share his story in my next
book. Here it is.

Early 1980s
North Hollywood, California

I tucked our little two-year-old into bed and
turned off the lights. My wife was already
asleep. We lived in the coziest little house in
North Hollywood, California. I had already
made up my mind to leave the entertainment
business. I had spent a good part of my life as
a tour manager for various musicians, and now
that we had a little girl, leaving home for a six-
week tour was more than a little uncomfortable. Once, when I had returned from a
three-week tour, she wouldn't even come
to me and reacted as if I was a stranger.

As I pondered these thoughts, I drifted off
into a peaceful sleep, only to be awakened very
early by Karen Carpenter's voice singing a
capella in my right ear, "We're all alone now
and I'm singing this song to you." I immediately woke up. This seemed different from a
dream. The sound was so clear, so real. I didn't
hear it in my left ear, only in the right, and it
felt as if Karen's lips were but half an inch
from my right ear. I could almost feel the
breath behind the words. To say I was startled
doesn't even begin to explain my reaction. This
didn't feel like any dream I had ever had, and
I dream a lot. My heart was racing. I woke
up my wife, Debbie, and asked if she heard

anything. It was just before 6:00 A.M. She
listened to my story and seemed puzzled as
to why Karen Carpenter's voice would come
to me in dreams. There was no way I could get
back to sleep, so I took a shower but couldn't
get this experience to leave me. It was beautiful and peaceful and I knew it was meant just
for me.

I came back into the bedroom and turned
on the television at a very low volume. The
lead story came across: Karen Carpenter had
suffered a massive heart attack and died at her
parent's home in Downey, California. I was in
shock. I stood there looking at my wife and
she said, "Oh my God, she came to you." I
had worked for Karen and Richard Carpenter
a few years earlier as a sound engineer and tour
manager. This very personal experience has
touched me in a way I cannot describe, and
is still with me to this day.

This experience, along with others throughout my life, prompted me to visit a medium
after my wife Debbie had returned home from
a reading with Jenny Crawford. I had only met
Jenny briefly a week earlier when Reverend
Sandy Moore introduced us at a fund-raiser
that was held at our home in Laguna Hills.
During that brief meeting I was struck by the
warmth and natural compassion exhibited by
both these ladies. I had known Sandy for
almost a year, as the founder of Tara's Angels
Center for Universal Truth, and as co-owner of
the famous Tara's Angels Store. Jenny was in

Southern California conducting readings and
holding seminars. Between her warmth and
compassion and my wife's enthusiasm after her
reading, I was set to see Jenny on the following
Saturday morning.

I am glad the reading was on tape because
something very unusual happened. About
halfway through the session Jenny explained
that someone very special was there to talk
to me. I had already heard from each of my
grandmothers and they certainly had loads to
say and I was grateful for their messages. Jenny
explained that the lady waiting patiently was
Karen Carpenter. Karen came through with
a few personal messages. Then, Jenny said,
"Karen wants to tell you something about
your teeth," that I needed some type of
dental work. I had just seen the dentist in
Palm Springs the prior week and had been
given a clean bill. I told Jenny how Karen
had great teeth. Maybe that's the message that
was coming through. Jenny said Karen was
shaking her head and saying no, laughing, and
pointing back to my front tooth. I was lost,
I had no idea what was going on. Jenny said
not to worry, that Karen had more to say and
would come to me in dream state. Other than
the confusion over my teeth, it was a wonderful reading and a joy to meet Jenny Crawford.

That very night, at 4:00 A.M., I woke from
a very compelling dream where I was in a position of responsibility, working under Richard
Carpenter. In this position, I felt immense
pressure. I had to succeed in my given area of

expertise or I would be letting Richard and
everyone who worked on the project down.
In the dream, the pressure was unbearable.
I couldn't wait to get out of that situation.

While still working, Karen looked over at
me and said, "How would you like to live
under that kind of pressure every day?"

I said, "No way, not ever!"

Then she showed me a visual image of a
shell-like object, misshapen and visually not
complete. She explained to me that it was a
soul who hadn't given itself the most important gift in the universe—self-love. She
explained that now she understood; it doesn't
matter if we're not appreciated by mothers or
brothers or understood by critics, because we
all have the ability to fill our souls with self-
love. If we don't get it elsewhere, we must give
it to ourselves. It sounds so simple and it is.
This self-love sustains our physical life. If we're
not getting love or feeling appreciated at home
or in the workplace, it is our responsibility to
give ourselves the necessary "stuff" that makes
us whole—self-love.

Then Karen said, "Oh, by the way, your
tooth . . . don't you remember Scotland?" She
chuckled and at that moment I awoke. My
heart was racing; what a dream! Everything
made such sense. And the Scotland memory?
I was there with Karen in 1976 and while on
tour I had an accident and broke my front
tooth in half! That's what Karen had been trying to tell me. She had sent me to her dentist
in Downey, California, but I had never gone

back to have the tooth permanently repaired.
Thank you, Karen Carpenter, and thank you,
Jenny Crawford, for being the intercessor!
    With love,
          Michael Lansing

I am grateful that Michael was happy to share the tender and precious moment of his visitation from Karen
Carpenter. Often many people do not know what to
expect when visiting a medium, and I am thankful that
when Michael came to see me he did so with an open
heart and mind.

4

What to Expect When Visiting a Medium

Everything I need to know is revealed to me.
Everything I need to know comes to me. All
is well in my life.

Heal Your Body
—Louise L. Hay

*W*hen you feel drawn to make a link with a loved one in the spirit world, I suggest that you contact a medium. Often you may feel drawn to an appointment time that coincides with an anniversary or significant date that relates to a loved one in the spirit world. You may find yourself feeling a strong urge to call a medium for an appointment that has been pre-orchestrated by your loved one in your sleep state.

Most people who call in a professional tradesperson for repairs on their home prefer someone who has been highly recommended to them, and the same principle applies when choosing a medium. Most reputable mediums never need to advertise, as word of mouth is sufficient. A true medium should be treated as a professional, and those who genuinely wish to make a loving connection with the spirit world will fit their schedule in and around the appointment time allocated by the medium.

Make sure when you arrive at the medium's house or office that you feel comfortable and safe within the immediate surroundings. If not, you should be honest and tell the medium that you feel uneasy in the environment; this may prompt them to make changes that improve conditions for other people. If you are in the right place, you will feel warmth and light engulf you immediately.

I recall one woman who came to see me, telling me of her first encounter with a medium. She was very nervous about the meeting, and upon entering the medium's property she saw the grass was overgrown and the grounds were very untidy. She said she felt a cold chill run down the back of her neck. There was a very old house on the property that seemed to be in disrepair. She tried to ignore her surroundings as she walked toward the front door of the house; and as she nervously knocked, it creaked open.

"Oh my God," she thought. "This is really making me nervous," and with her hand shaking, she leaned forward to knock again.

As she did so, she heard an old lady's croaky voice call out, "Come in."

This was all too much for my client, and she explained to me that the experience frightened her. She stood shaking, wondering whether to go into the house or run away. She decided to look for a positive sign as to whether she should go in, and just at that very moment a black cat brushed past her legs. "That's it," she said, and she was off. She ran as quickly as she could to her car.

"I never looked back," she told me. "It felt like I was at the Addams family home!"

The medium should make you feel at ease and comfortable the moment you meet. The room where you receive your reading would ideally be light and bright, and you need to have eye contact with the medium, so neither party should be wearing dark glasses.

This is a very serious and responsible business, and you are seeking a genuine medium to give you a reading. Remember, our eyes are the mirrors of our soul, and this is where our true emotions emerge from.

Make sure you do not offer any personal information to the medium. People pass general comments when entering new surroundings and body language can be easily read by a skilled medium. Sometimes un-genuine readers can hold on to these comments and play on the emotions and vulnerability of a sad person.

I recommend that you are not completely discon-nected or "switched off" from the medium, as a gen-uine reader is not to be exploited. It is important for a medium to hear your voice during the reading. Even a "yes" or "no" will suffice, as hearing the vibration of your voice will draw your loved one's energy in closer to speak with the medium. Many people are not aware of the healing vibration a medium channels to them.

Try to be open and receptive. Good mediums will sound positive, giving you positive and clear informa-tion, and you will feel a loving energy radiating from them. Most will give warnings if they come up in a reading, and if the medium is attuned to a higher vibra-tional level, this information will be explained to you in a spiritual manner. The messages given to you ought to be easily understood and precise, and the medium should not mind your asking questions throughout the reading. It is advisable, however, to wait until the end of a reading, for some mediums may have already answered your questions by then.

When visiting a medium, it is crucial that the infor-mation given to you is being gathered from the higher planes where our loved ones reside. There have been reported incidents where a medium may start a reading positively, passing on significant messages, and a few moments later divert or slip onto a negative vibrational plane, offering devastating and upsetting news for the client. Our higher self does not carry an ego, and mediums should not allow their ego to take over, to direct the conversation toward themselves. Some people have told me that their reading with a medium was wonderful for the first twenty minutes, but for the remainder of the reading, the medium switched to telling her/his own life story.

The medium should be expected to act professionally, realizing that the client has come to seek guidance, reassurance, and valuable information regarding his or her own personal life pathway. When it comes to fees, there is no set amount that is typically charged. I believe the spirit world endeavors to provide for spiritual workers, and a friend of ours always says, "Where God guides, God provides, and so it is." It is worth mentioning that many mediums happily do a portion of their spiritual work without any monetary gain to ensure that those who are in need are not turned away.

At times I have found the spirit world may provide the most important piece of information in the last few minutes of the session. Like other occupations, we mediums all have our good and bad days. It is not necessarily that we receive a bad connection from the spirit world, but the medium may be tired, ill, or run down at the time of your connection, and may not always hear and see clearly.

Many a good medium has only lasted twelve months in this occupation, because they have worked themselves to a level of exhaustion, and become burned out. Sadly so, I have met such people, and it has taken them years to recover and regain their vital energy levels. This reinforces the message that mediums need to pace themselves carefully. It is extremely important to eat a healthy diet, exercise regularly, get plenty of fresh air, and drink lots of purified water.

Most mediums will offer to tape-record your reading because they trust the information they are receiving and relaying to you. This is a good idea because important messages can be misinterpreted or missed at the time of your reading. It is helpful to be able to review the reading later.

I conduct a reading session by sitting opposite my client, and before I begin the reading I close my eyes and say the Lord's Prayer, asking for upliftment and protection during our time of communication. Praying helps to raise my vibration to a higher level, which is like turning on a switch with my energy field.

I focus my energy and attention to the top of my head, which is known as the crown chakra area. I visualize this area opening up like a flower with a golden light shining upon it, and when I have finished communicating with the spirit world, I visualize this flower above my head closing up again.

I prefer to read for people about whom I have no knowledge or information; then the messages given can provide strong evidence and proof to my client of life after death.

While connecting with the spirit world in a reading, I remain fully conscious and speak in a normal, natural voice. If there is an interruption during the session, I am able to deal with the disturbance as the spirit waits patiently until the communication can begin again.

I want to make my clients feel at ease and relaxed during our time together, so I work in a very simplistic manner. During this initial settling down period, I feel the spirits start to gather around me. It is as though they are taking a good look at me as they draw in closer to make contact with the client. The communication I make with the spirit world is similar to having a friendly conversation with a person, although the spirit I am talking to is visible and audible to me in a spiritual sense, rather than physically.

Sometimes it takes a spirit a little time to adapt to the vibrational changes of our communication. Once this takes place and my energy level is raised to the same frequency wave as theirs, then I can hear their messages clearly.

I always leave room in a reading for a person to ask questions or tell me if they do not understand. The spirit works very hard to make this connection, and each moment of contact with the spirit world is very precious.

It is easier for the spirits to make contact if they had an understanding about spiritual awareness and life after death before they passed over. Sometimes when a spirit is anxious to make a communication with a loved one, they will pop in, so to speak, or visit me prior to the person coming for a reading. I feel a strong presence around me, and on some occasions the spirit will speak to me, giving me their name. I will generally hear this information in a voice that sounds like a whisper. The spirit will just fade in and out while waiting to make the vital connection with a loved one.

When a spirit wants to make contact with you, they will open the door for this communication to take place. This happened when I met Jack in Southern California in August, 2000. Jack's friend Teresa and another woman were booked to see me for private readings. As it turned out, Teresa's friend wasn't able to make the appointment, so she asked Jack to come along instead. Jack later explained to me that he did not really know what to expect when visiting a medium. Before they arrived at the home where I was working, the spirit of a young man appeared in front of me. I knew he was looking for either Jack or Teresa, as I could tell he was anxiously awaiting their visit.

After meeting them both, it very quickly transpired that it was Jack's son waiting to communicate with him. As I told him later, I could see his son standing beside him and Jack seemed dazed during our reading.

Later, I received a letter from Jack, written on October 8, 2001:

> Dear Jenny,
>
> I would like to thank you for opening my eyes and my heart. My friend Teresa took me to see you last August 14 for a private session. The loss of my only child, my son, was devastating to me. Not only was I his father, but a buddy, a roommate, and a mother, too. Raising him myself from the age of nine to his death at eighteen-and-a-half was probably the greatest responsibility, but also the most rewarding one I have had or will ever have in my life.
>
> After his death, I felt totally alone. No wife and not being religious, my anger was directed at God. My depression was destroying me. I was drinking excessively, being drunk most of the time. I contemplated suicide and found myself in precarious situations. Friends directed me toward psychiatrists and bereavement groups. I felt somewhat out of place until finding a group that was only parents that have lost children. That was a great help at the time.
>
> Finally, after a year and a half, one day I woke up, shaved off my beard, and started

putting my life back together again. I put
on a very good front, going through life like
a normal person, but I was still hurting with
little relief. They say that time heals, well, [it
does] to some degree. My anger calmed and
my thoughts of suicide dwindled to just wanting God to take me soon.

Then came my visit to you. Right off the
bat after being seated before you, you stated to
me that when you opened the door, you saw
Teresa, myself, and a young man, a boy standing there. We had never met you before, and
I was in total shock at that opening statement.
That hit me as hard as when the doctor told
me that my son died. It was like time standing
still. For the next hour I probably remained
in shock for I could not believe all the things
you were saying to me that only my son and
I would know. After our goodbyes, my friend
Teresa noted my fumbling and unorganized
manner that day on our way home. During
the next week I reviewed the tape from the
session many times and recorded most of it
into longhand notes. From there I studied
all of that session.

From the session and the tape I felt such
an uplift that it was like feeling love again. I
still cry from time to time and my mind still
wanders, but it is in a more positive way.

You must understand I had no idea, no
idea what I was getting into when my friend
brought me to see you. I had always wished
for a sign from him but was never able to

connect. You did this for me with the session and the tape. I thank you with all of my heart for how I feel now.

With love,

Jack Drea

P.S. I waited till this day to write you, for this is the date my son entered the spirit world.

I thank Jack for opening up his heart and sharing his precious story.

When a loved one in the spirit world wishes to make contact, they always find a way. This happened when I met Cindy. I had only just started her reading when a man stepped in closely to me and asked me to bring Adam into the room. Cindy looked surprised, as she told me, "Adam is my husband and he is sitting outside in the car."

"Well, bring him in," the spirit requested, and I smiled as Adam nervously joined the reading. It was exciting to hear Adam's father identify himself from the spirit world, and pass on vital messages to his son. It was also pleasing to see Adam leave the reading with tears of joy in his eyes.

It is my wish that each person who has an encounter with a medium will walk away with a lasting and loving memory of an experience that they hold close to their heart forever—an experience that will leave little room for doubt that there is in fact, a life hereafter. If this has happened to you, I urge you to share the information with your family and friends. If you do share with people who are nonbelieving or skeptics about life after death, you will be sowing vital seeds of thought toward their very own enlightenment.

Some people who have had an encounter with a medium leave this enlightening experience knowing their lives have truly been touched by an unforeseen power and light that will engulf them always. In a very short time after a reading, most people start to feel a vibrational change within themselves and their surroundings, creating a much happier, peaceful, and positive pathway.

To me, the true work of a medium is to link people with loved ones in the spirit world, passing on reassurance that their departed loved ones are now safe, well, and happy. Many people also ask me to pass on messages of love to those in the spirit world. Remember, the spirit does constantly hear your silent voice and loving thoughts.

My next story, "Mother's Day," reinstates this message of a mother in the spirit world who hears her children's messages of love and wishes to reply.

5

Mother's Day

"Everything can be bearable, when there
was *love*." This is perhaps the most important
fact when we are dealing with the death of a
parent. With the exception of tiny infants,
every child will mourn the loss of a mother
or father, even when they are grown and
parents themselves.

On Life After Death
—Elisabeth Kübler-Ross

A prayer of hope, a letter of love, and lots of
faith reinforced my own belief in the power
of our loving mothers to touch us from the spirit
world.

Our mothers are so precious to us and where
would any of us be without the advice, love, and
support of a dear mom. But it seemed as though my
whole world was turned upside down when I received news of my own beloved mother's sudden
passing. I had just begun a book tour in California
to promote my first book, *Through the Eyes of Spirit*.

On the day my mother's funeral service was taking place in New Zealand, I was conducting a workshop in Southern California with my husband Robert. I drew upon all my beliefs as a medium and knew in my heart that my darling mom had now found a new haven of peace and tranquility in the spirit world. I asked God to make me a strong person as I continued to be an instrument in helping others to deal with their grief.

At the workshop, I was handed a letter by a lady named Corinn Codye, who did the technical editing on *Through the Eyes of Spirit*. Corinn came up to me at the meeting and said she had a very special letter to share with me. She reached inside her jacket pocket and produced a plain white, weathered and torn envelope. As she opened the letter to show me, it rather took me by surprise, as the contents contained loving messages from a family that had recently lost their mother. The messages were from a close and loving family to their mother, Louann, telling her how much they missed and loved her. It seemed that this letter had been sent from Newport Beach, California, tied to several colored balloons. It had traveled over the freeway and over an ocean and mountain range and had landed inland in the small rural town of Pinon Hills, nearly a hundred miles away from its point of origin.

The letter had been found on Corinn's property by her teenaged twin boys, who were playing in an area of wooded ground that stretched for two acres. The boys noticed some money lying on the ground, and

this caught their attention and drew them to discover
the envelope, which was lying beside the money. We
had no idea how the money got there, as it had no connection to the letter lying beside it. However, it caught
their attention and drew them to the letter.

Corinn told me that she was going to write back to
the family, as they had given a forwarding address on
their letter. I asked her if she would also send a copy of
my book to the family, which she diligently did the
next day. She also enclosed my telephone number in
Laguna Beach, where I was staying at the time, which is
very close to Newport Beach.

It was only a few days later that I received a phone
call from a woman called Nancy, who had written the
letter along with other family members. I invited
Nancy to come and see me for a reading and explained
to her that I did not know whether or not her mother
would come through in her reading. Nancy was filled
with joy and apprehension as we spoke, and as our
meeting neared she started to become very emotional
and nervous. On the day of our appointment, she telephoned me and asked if it would be all right to bring
her husband Denis with her, which of course I agreed
to at once.

I felt deep within my heart that a beautiful sequence
of events was happening here. A family had posted a
letter to their mother in the spirit world, sent it up into
the big sky attached to several balloons, and it had
reached me, someone who has a link with the spirit

world. It seemed truly magical, and as the hour arrived for Nancy's reading, I was sure that her mother had orchestrated this meeting.

As I walked to the gate to greet Nancy and Denis, I was overwhelmed by their beautiful presence and angelic light. They both stood tall and walked with such grace and light around them. Nancy was very nervous and tentative about our meeting, and I could tell her emotions were running wild. Before I could speak, she had tears streaming down her shiny cheeks. I sat Nancy and Denis down and explained the way I work as a medium. I also told them that I could equally sympathize with them, as my own mother had just passed over four weeks prior to our meeting.

I explained to Nancy and Denis that they might think this meeting today was perhaps a coincidence or mere chance. However, I felt very differently. I told them I believed this was a sheer gift of magic to bring forth our meeting and connection this day with the spirit world, and that God had played a strong and loving hand in this Divine intervention. After all, when you write a letter to your mom who has recently passed over and send it up on several balloons, do you really expect to receive a letter in return, a medium's book, and an invitation for a communication with the spirit world? Especially when the medium has only just arrived in the country and traveled all the way from New Zealand!

I explained to this special couple that I could not dial a telephone number and directly call their mothers up in the spirit world. I did reassure them both, however, that something very special could happen, as it seemed Nancy's mother had gone to a great deal of trouble to connect us and arrange this meeting. It did help our possibilities for a good connection to know that both Nancy and Denis shared a strong love for their mothers.

As I switched on my recorder to tape the reading and began to tune in, I prayed very hard that this couple would not be disappointed and that my link with the spirit world would be strong that day. It was not long before I felt a strong motherly presence around us. I could see a lady who had been very unwell prior to her passing, but she seemed to be very bright and angelic as she stepped in closer.

It truly seemed that Nancy and Denis had been guided to meet me. Apparently, Denis' mother had also passed over around the same time as mine. They had been trying to conceive their first child for six years, and on the day of his mother's passing, Nancy conceived. Their story was becoming more and more interesting all the time.

As I looked across to Nancy and Denis, all I could see were two beautiful and clear faces looking back at me. Their eyes were wide open and they displayed such peaceful vibrations, these two darling souls who had been brought to me as a channel to try to bring reassurance and comfort to them that both their mothers were now safe and well in the spirit world.

Nancy's eyes filled with tears as I started to tune in strongly, and she too became aware of her mother's presence. During such times, it is important for me to hear my client's voice occasionally, as the sound of that voice encourages a loved one from the spirit world to step in closer. However, I always caution my clients not to give me any personal details or information about themselves or loved ones, for only in this way will they truly know the connection with the spirit world is genuine.

Nancy's mother, Louann, came in closer and more strongly upon hearing Nancy's voice, and she continued to give messages of proof: important and pertinent descriptions, and expressions of love and support. For instance, she described a diamond cross that Nancy had at home in her jewelry box. As the mother continued to give me details and information, the tears trickled down her daughter's face. Nancy even laughed and cried at the same time as she experienced such joy and relief in talking with her mother once again.

Nancy told me that when she lost her mother, it was as though her right arm had been torn off. Then her mother stepped in closer again and thanked her daughter for the love and support she had given and for staying in the hospital with her during her illness and last moments. "She held my hand till the end," her mother told me, and she again thanked her daughter. I could see that Nancy was a loving and caring daughter, and that this was a precious, heavenly time for them both, as mother and daughter could share a communication together once again.

Though many people may be aware of this fact, when a love link is strong I feel it is possible for a person to speak directly to a spirit in their mind, and it is not always necessary to be in the presence of a medium. However, sometimes a direct communication can be difficult if the person who has lost a loved one is grieving deeply, for this grief cloud can prevent a communication on a one-on-one level. This is when it is helpful to consult a medium who can supply the needed energy link to bridge the communication gap, as in this case.

Denis' mother was also very active in our reading. She was a strong character while living on the earth plane and managed to make a good communication with us. Denis would nod his head and say, "Yes, that is correct," or "That is exactly what mom would say when she was alive."

His mother spoke about his business, their home together, and many other personal details. She offered reassurance and guidance to them both. She wanted to tell them she knew about the baby on the way and that she had found perfect peace in the spirit world. I could feel that this couple had their lives beautifully organized, and Nancy's mother stepped forward again to tell her how proud she was of her, telling me that Nancy was a guidance counselor.

Nancy and her family had sent up the precious letter to their mother, Louann, on Mother's Day, and as our reading came to a conclusion, she asked me a question. "Jenny, what do you think the real reason was for Mom getting in touch with us this way? Was she trying to tell us something else of great importance we need to know?"

The answer that came back was plain and simple; "Oh, my dear, your mother is telling you that she received your letter, and she also wishes to send her love back to you all. She wants you to know that she is now without pain and suffering and is at peace."

As this magical time with Nancy and Denis came to an end, I knew in my heart that I had been connected with two very special souls who would continue to spread love and light wherever they walked in life.

As we waved goodbye, I smiled to myself and marveled once again at the wonderful and mysterious way this couple had been brought to me, to have a loving communication with both their mothers in the spirit world. Although I am never surprised at the miraculous ways the spirit world works in making such valuable and loving connections, Nancy and Denis' story was rather unique. A beautiful gift of love had been returned this day

The words, "I received your letter," from Nancy's mother will stay in my heart forever, and I am sure this experience also changed their lives in a positive and heartwarming way. A letter of love was sent up into the Universe, and I believe that God guided this letter to the correct destination so that Nancy, Denis, and their family could receive a reply that would bring them peace and a new understanding of where their mothers now reside.

Two months after Nancy and Denis' reading, I received the most wonderful card from them, which said:

> *I believe in Angels . . .*
> *That are always hovering near,*
> *Whispering encouragement*
> *Whenever clouds appear,*
> *Protecting us from danger*
> *And showing us the way,*
> *Performing little miracles*
> *Within our lives each day . . . .*

Dearest Jenny,

    That's what you did—perform a little miracle by being yourself "a gift—an Angel."

    Meeting with you changed our lives. We will never forget how incredible the experience was. We both can't thank you enough for your kindness and thoughtfulness. It meant more to us than words can express.

    Looking forward to our continued friendship. Much love and happiness always,

            Nancy and Denis

Two years later, Rob and I met Nancy, Denis, and Corinn at a wonderful Italian restaurant in Newport Beach, where the waiters sang to the guests.

We were all happy to meet one another again, and as the five of us sat down at a circular table together, a male waiter with the most wonderful voice began singing "Ave Maria." We all looked teary-eyed as we felt like a special family, reunited once again.

6

Platform Work

THE LONDON PALLADIUM
I should have been beside myself with
excitement, of course, but all I could think
of was "Oh heavens—that means I've got to
do it. I've really got to go on at the London
Palladium!"

> *Whispering Voices*
> —Doris Stokes,
> International Medium

Although much of my work is done in private sessions, I also frequently stand in front of large groups of people, giving clairvoyant messages to individuals. I call this platform work. The word platform reminds me of a railway station, and it sometimes feels this way, as many spirits line up to make contact with their loved ones in the audience.

I trust when I am giving a clairvoyant demonstration that my built-in telephone exchange to the spirit world will not cross too many wires, as the spirits often gather together in a group and start talking to me all at once.

When I am working in front of audiences and giving a clairvoyant demonstration, the spirit world homes in toward a collective beacon of light that radiates from the crowd. It is this guiding light of love that draws the spirits toward the medium to make contact with those in the audience.

When giving clairvoyant demonstrations, mediums endeavor to keep the energy flowing; hearing an audience laugh lifts the vibration of our connection, allowing stronger communication with the spirit world.

It would be wonderful if clairvoyants could rehearse their performances before giving a public demonstration. Unfortunately, it does not work this way, and we often have to wait until we are standing in front of an audience before the messages start to flow forth.

It is good practice to not chat with any members of the audience prior to a meeting, as this may draw suspicion upon the authenticity of our work. I always aim to make sure my messages are strong and clear, striving to give those in the audience as much proof of the life hereafter as possible.

I recall being asked to do some clairvoyant work at an evening called "Meet the Mediums" at one of our local theaters. I felt privileged to be invited by a well-known medium, Maureen Chapman, who has been my colleague and one of my spiritual teachers over the years. As we sat backstage, the theater began to fill up; you could hear all the excitement building in the audience as people were being seated. I glanced through the side curtain, and could not believe how many people were starting to gather. The organizer of the meeting came backstage and told us they were bringing in more chairs, as already there were over 650 people in the theater. I knew we were in for a wonderful evening of clairvoyance.

Maureen and I walked onto the stage and were introduced to the audience. We had taken pride in dressing up for the spirit world this night, and it was fun wearing some sparkle and glitter. Maureen started the evening off with a demonstration of her clairvoyant ability. I sat behind the stage in the wings awaiting my turn, and could hear the audience with all their "oohs and ahs," as Maureen continued to rattle off message after message, supplying Christian names, middle names, nicknames, and many valuable pieces of information to those who were receiving messages. The audience laughed out loud several times, and on one occasion she had them almost rolling in the aisles.

Maureen said, "I would like to come to the gentleman sitting in the middle of the theater," and promptly a microphone was handed to him.

"I warn you," he called out to Maureen, "I am one of your biggest skeptics."

The crowd laughed out loud and another gentleman at the back of the hall called out even louder.

"You can't be, I am!"

This brought another roar of laughter from the audience.

Maureen went on to give the first skeptic his message. "I can see you and your spouse having a dispute over chopping a tree down," she said into the microphone.

The gentleman called back, "How do you know that?"

With that, his spouse chipped in and said, "Yes, I do not want the tree cut down, but he will not listen."

The audience kept chuckling as the message continued. Maureen went on to bring this gentleman's grandfather through from the spirit world. She gave clear and precise details, and once again the gentleman called back, but this time in a different tone.

"How do you know so much about my grandpappy?" he asked. "Do you know, I think you have just about won me over!" The audience clapped and laughed.

Maureen then directed her attention to the skeptical man at the back of the theater, and when she gave him a lot of good clear messages, he too admitted that there was definitely something in this life-hereafter stuff.

This reminds me of a story I heard about a woman who nagged her skeptical husband to attend a clairvoyant demonstration with her. As they sat together in a crowded theater, a medium stepped onto the platform to give messages to the audience. The medium stood there without saying a word, and the woman's husband burst into laughter.

He said to his wife, "How can anyone concentrate with all that din going on? Fancy bringing in a band of musicians at this time."

The woman was embarrassed and quickly told her husband to be quiet. To which he replied, "How can anyone be quiet with all those musicians playing their instruments so loud."

The woman looked puzzled, as she could not see or hear any musicians.

At that moment, the medium began her address by saying, "Ladies and gentlemen, before I proceed, I must apologize as I was distracted by a band from the spirit world coming into the theater to play their music. I was just waiting for them to leave before I began."

The woman's husband sat with his mouth wide open, as it appeared he and the medium were the only ones in the theatre who saw and heard the spiritual music.

The evening was moving along beautifully with Maureen, and as I sat backstage, I asked the spirit world to give me a message to start me off quickly. At that moment I felt a young man step in closely.

"My name is Barry," he told me, "and I was killed in a motor accident. My mom is here, sitting in the front row of the audience." As I walked on stage, all I could see were many faces looking toward me from every direction.

Generally, before a clairvoyance demonstration, I need to speak for a few moments, and the spirit world tells me when they are ready to communicate. When working in front of large crowds, there are many spirits gathered in the background waiting to make contact with loved ones in the audience.

That night I heard a strong voice in the back of my head saying, "Come on, we are ready." I felt it was Barry back again, so I looked to the front row of the audience and announced that I had a Barry linked to me from the spirit world. A woman quickly raised her hand. She looked overwhelmed.

"This is your son, darling," I said to her.

"Yes," she cried out, with her hand over her face.

"Your son tells me he was killed in a motor accident," I said.

"Yes, that is correct," she said. The messages continued, and I could see that the love link between mother and son was distinctly strong; in fact, I wanted to stay with this dear woman all night, giving her messages. However, that was not possible, as an older woman from the spirit world quickly stepped in closer to communicate.

"I am looking for my daughter Stella in the audience; she is at the back of the theater," she told me. Stella put her hand up and as the microphone came to her, she claimed her mother's messages.

"Stella is my nickname," she told us. "Mom always called me by this name."

Her mother went on to give her another message, and then gave a message to Stella's daughter and sister sitting beside her. They were sitting so far back in the audience that I could only just see the outlines of their faces, but I could tell by their voices that they were happy with their messages.

The spirit world knows when family members are together in an audience. They need not be sitting beside one another, as the spirit world will know exactly where they are seated. Sometimes acquaintances in an audience can also be connected when giving out a message.

My next message was interesting as it was directed to a woman in the front row. I could see she had recently moved into a new apartment, and I commented on how nice her new landlord was. When conveying this message to her, my attention was drawn to a blue light flickering above the head of a gentleman sitting at the back of the theater. I asked the gentleman if he would come forward to the front of the theater, and asked the woman if she knew this gentleman. She blushed as she said, "Yes, this is my new landlord."

The audience let out a shriek of laughter.

Just then another spirit gentleman, Alan, stepped in. I was finding it hard to connect him with the person whom he was seeking in the audience. "Who are you looking for, Alan?" I asked, and fortunately, with that he said, "Susan, I am looking for Susan. She is sitting at the back of the theater, by the side light."

As I pointed to this area, where one of the theater lights was shining, a woman called out, "Yes, I am Susan." She received a lovely message.

I was finding it hard to keep up with the spirits who were stepping in, as they all were very eager to speak to family, friends, and loved ones. Another spirit stepped in and asked to speak with Bo, a woman in the crowd I managed to locate. Another spirit announced, "My name is Steven," and he showed me a small blue light flickering above the head of a man who appeared to be in his early thirties.

The blue light is sometimes all I can see of a spirit moving about the audience. It seemed these two young gentlemen had been school chums, and Steven was very grateful for this friendship all those years ago.

I could see the initial D being written above the top of the man's head in the audience. I was having difficulty catching the name, and the man in the audience said:

"My name is Dean."

"Well, Dean, Steven is giving you a message, and of course we try not to give out any messages that are too personal in public, however, he wants you to know that you are going to meet a lovely lady very soon, and your personal life is going to be very good."

Dean called out, "Oh good, it's about time," to which the audience laughed and clapped at the same time.

As the audience laughter slowly stopped an elderly spirit woman stepped in beside me, and told me she was looking for her son Cyril in the audience. A gentleman who looked to be in his early sixties raised his hand. I found it interesting to see a green and orange parrot from the spirit world flying around him. The audience chuckled again. It transpired that his mother had been in a nursing home for some years, and her sixty-year-old pet parrot also lived there with her. Cyril's mother passed over at the age of ninety-nine and the very next day her pet parrot just curled up and died. The parrot could not live without her. I found it intriguing that after spending so many years together, the parrot and Cyril's mom were reunited so quickly after her passing.

The spirit of a little girl appeared to me next, looking for her mother in the audience, and standing beside the little girl in the spirit world was a small golden-colored dog. The little girl told me that she passed over with leukemia and interestingly enough, only moments after she stopped breathing, her dog died for no apparent reason. I explained to the audience that sometimes we take our pets with us. Her mother was so grateful to hear from her darling wee daughter, and many people in the audience sat quietly wiping their eyes as her message was delivered.

After hearing such touching stories, I always pray for the grief-stricken people in the audience, and feel encouraged that some of them leave such meetings feeling as though they are wrapped in a golden blanket of protection, filled with healing, love, and light.

Spirits were lining up around me fast, and just then two men from the same family came forward, telling me they had both died in individual drowning accidents, and directing me toward their aunt sitting in the audience.

My attention was then drawn toward the middle of the theater, where I could see a beautiful baby boy being held above a woman's head—the baby was floating like an angel. I pointed to a young woman several rows from the stage. Understandably, she was too upset to speak, so I asked her if she would come up and see me when the meeting had concluded. The spirit world wished to give her love and reassurance that her baby was safe and well.

After feeling the woman's sadness, I smiled to myself when the next message came through from spirit. It was from an elderly gentleman named Edward, who asked me to wait, and wait I did, as he walked ever so slowly toward me to continue his communication. While I waited, I located his daughter in the audience. She was laughing so hard, and she said this was typical of her father when he was alive, he would just walk in a slow shuffle and everyone had to wait for him.

More messages flowed through, and as our demonstration came to an end, I could feel that all those attending had especially enjoyed their evening of clairvoyance. It made me feel so proud and humble to be part of such a wonderful sharing of love, healing, and kindness.

As we said good night, Maureen and I were overwhelmed with the number of people who quickly rushed up on stage to speak with us. We seemed to be standing and talking for ages when I noticed the stage lights being turned off, and I took this as a sign from the organizers that it was time to go home.

Just as I was about to walk off the stage, a young girl came up to me. She was approximately ten years of age, with beautiful dark hair and big brown eyes.

"Excuse me," she said in a soft, gentle voice.

"Yes, darling," I said, as I turned to look at her. I could tell from the onset, she was a special little soul.

"Can you tell me, please," she said, as her big brown eyes filled with tears, "if animals really do go on in to the spirit world, like humans?"

I replied quickly and firmly, "Oh yes, of course they do, darling. Our animals go on to heaven and are cared for by our loved ones in the spirit world."

"Well," she said, "it's just that my bird died, and I wondered if it was safe."

Interestingly enough, even though I thought I had run out of breath and messages for the evening, I was shown an elderly woman named Joyce, who was holding on to a beautiful white bird, just like a dove.

"Oh my dear," I said to the young girl, "you have a grandmother Joyce in spirit who was very close to you, and she is holding on to a beautiful white bird."

The young girl's eyes filled with tears, as she said, "Yes, that's my grandmother, and my bird was white." A smile emerged on her face as she skipped away happily, and I thought to myself, what a magical way to end an evening of clairvoyance.

I believe that those attending such meetings go away feeling a strong sense of healing and an overflow of loving messages.

At another meeting I gave a message to a woman in the audience who was remarried after having lost her first spouse as a result of a motorbike accident. Her departed spouse stepped in closely, and I could actually see him standing very clearly behind her. He was a tall, well-built young man, who had a lovely crop of thick, dark, curly hair. He told me that he had been struck by a truck and that the accident was not his fault. As I relayed these messages to his spouse, she seemed disinterested and hardly responded to the message. Sometimes a medium must give someone a message that really hits them between the eyes before getting a response, and what came next gained her attention.

Her spouse wanted me to tell her that he had her dog with him in the spirit world, a black Labrador. With this the woman cried out, "Oh my God." She then shared with us that she got the dog after her spouse was killed, to help ease the heartache and emotional pain. Just recently the dog had met with a painful and tragic death and so this message gave her peace of mind and consoled her deeply. I felt happy that her spouse in spirit was able to get this message to her, and furthermore that she now believed her spouse was safe and well in the spirit world.

Another time I was giving a talk and clairvoyant demonstration to some students at a massage school in Nevada City, California. The students varied in age, and as I got up to speak, I felt the beautiful healing energy that had been created by this special group.

The students had never before seen anyone give a clairvoyant demonstration, and I could feel their excitement as they all sat, watching me intently.

One message that came through was very interesting, as I was given a date, August 27. A young man named Jason put his hand up and claimed the message.

"Yes," he said, "that was my Mom's birthday."

His mother in the spirit world went on to give Joe several messages, and then said she really wanted Jason to start enjoying every Christmas. She wanted her son to place a bright star at the top of his Christmas tree and remember as he looked at this star that she was now at peace. The tears flowed down Jason's cheeks as his Mom shared that she had committed suicide prior to his eighteenth birthday and before Christmas. He was now thirty-one years of age and had not enjoyed a Christmas since her passing. He came up to me after the meeting and hugged me, telling me that this message had turned his whole life around. I felt very humble to be an instrument in relaying such a simple but profound message.

Many others at the school received messages, and as I said my goodbyes to these special people I hoped that some day we would meet again.

While staying in San Clemente, California, I was invited to do some workshops with groups of people in their homes. A woman named Tina invited Rob and me to her home to do some workshops. Her home was warm and full of life and laughter, providing good energy in which to work. While giving clairvoyance at one of the meetings, an older woman named Dorothy stepped forward from the spirit world, telling me her daughter was at the meeting. The daughter put her hand up at the back of the room.

"Yes, my mother's name is Dorothy," she said.

I am not sure whether she felt it really was her mom, but what came next thoroughly convinced her. As I walked toward her daughter, Dorothy wanted me to say in a loud and clear voice, "Well, hello, hello, hello."

Her daughter put her hand up to her face, as once again her mother asked me to say, "Well, hello, hello, hello."

"Oh my," her daughter said, "that is exactly how mom used to announce herself, I cannot believe it." I was thankful that Dorothy's introduction was authentic, giving proof to her daughter that her spirit was alive and well.

The energy transmitted by working in front of an audience while demonstrating platform work contributes toward strong and loving messages being conveyed from the spirit world. Regardless of whether a person has received a message, they have been linked to a powerful, loving, and healing connection, and I am sure many people walk away from such events knowing that their lives have been touched by spirit.

7

Touched by Spirit

It's a very important time because you are
here for a very special purpose which is yours
and yours alone. If you live well, you will
never have to worry about dying.

You can do that even if you have only one
day to live.

To live well means basically to learn to
love.

"Faith, love and hope, but the biggest of
the three is love."

On Life After Death
—Elisabeth Kübler-Ross

Over the years I have met many people who have
experienced heartrending situations in their lives.
A lot of pain and hurt is brought about by the loss of
a loved one, and at some point during our lifetime
we all will suffer the loss of a close family member. It
takes courage and stamina for the bereaved to regain
strength, and to continue with their lives here on
earth.

Most parents are conditioned to believe that they
will pass over prior to their children, and a shock

wave sets in when their children die before them. One of the worst nightmares that could happen to a person in life is the loss of a child; this is the saddest situation that could possibly happen to any loving parent. Life will never be the same again for them, as part of their heart is intertwined with their child. Death is one element of our existence that is totally unpredictable, a person may leave the earth plane at any given time. Even though our children may go on before us, the spiritual link between loving hearts can never be severed.

When working with people who have suffered tremendous tragedies in their lives, I can feel their emotional pain and anguish. I find myself getting a lump in my throat—this happened to me one day when I saw a mother whose daughter had been strangled by her exhusband. The mother wished to ask her daughter in the spirit world some questions; unfortunately, she was too distraught to do so. The only way the mother could communicate the questions she wished to ask was to write them down on paper. Her throat was closed with grief as she struggled to speak.

When souls are taken in such tragic circumstances it can hinder their communication with a medium. Sometimes it takes an extensive amount of work before the spirit is healed and able to make contact through a medium.

The following short stories are about people I have read for. Each story holds a different message, and once again reinstates the painful experiences people endure through life. They also bring forth messages of joy and happiness, as connections are made between themselves and loved ones in the spirit world, where divine harmony and peace is found. Among these stories are parents who have lost children. My heart bleeds for them, and I always pray they gain healing from the spirit world during our sessions together.

The Unthinkable Happened

It took Judy three years to gather the courage to visit me for a reading after her daughter Nicky was tragically killed in a car accident.

Approximately twelve months after Judy's reading, she sent me a heartfelt letter.

Judy has opened up her heart and soul to share her story, in the hope that other bereaved parents may gain reassurance and solace from her experience in making contact with her daughter in the spirit world. Judy is a teacher, and also counsels bereaved parents.

Judy's Letter

Dear Jenny,

In April 1992 the unthinkable happened. Nicky, the second of my three daughters, was killed in a car accident. My whole life was completely turned upside down and inside out by the impact of this tragedy. It was as if the sun had lost its shine and the birds had lost their song. The depth of my sorrow and despair was beyond belief.

At twenty-five, Nicky was an attractive, vivacious young woman working as a speech language therapist. A committed Christian, she was also very involved in youth work and used her special talent for drama and puppetry to present her own message of faith to young people. She touched so many people, young and old, in a very special and positive way.

For me, personally, she was my cornerstone, my soul mate beyond any boundaries of space or time. As a busy mother, grandmother, teacher, counselor, and advocate, I was continually giving of myself emotionally and always, just as my reserves were running low, there would be Nicky, with a phone call, a letter, or a "homecoming," to restore my soul with her love, her wit, and her special sparkle.

In the days, weeks, and months following her death I was like a wounded lioness licking my wounds as I reluctantly forced myself back into my usual life pattern, a shadow of my former self. I was back at work, back to helping people, and trying to help my three surviving children cope with their grief struggles. Outwardly, I probably appeared to be coping well. Inwardly I was empty, desolate, and very, very lonely. Many times I thought of going to see Jenny, a medium who had been recommended to me by another grieving parent and dear friend. Each time, however, I decided against it, partly because of my daughter's Christian beliefs. I thought that because she would have, in life, rejected the idea of spiritual contact, so in death she would not make contact, and partly out of fear that it would all be a sham, and I would be left even more bereft than before.

However, things began to happen that made me believe that somehow my daughter was intervening in my life in very positive ways, and I began to feel compelled to try and make contact. At last, after three years, I made my appointment with Jenny. It was to be a momentous decision.

I approached Jenny's door in a state of great apprehension and was welcomed into a quiet, restful room with an all-pervading sense of peace. Jenny's face radiated a glow of serene beauty, and I began to feel much more at ease. There was no artifice, no hocus-pocus, just this lovely, friendly, genuine woman who sat opposite me. After a few words of reassurance she turned on the tape deck, closed her eyes, breathed deeply, and then began speaking in a normal, natural voice.

From that moment on, the downward spiral of my life stopped in its tracks. The contact, first with my mother (who had died nineteen years before) and then with my daughter, was clear and absolutely, indisputably real. The tears flowed down my cheeks and my spirits soared as proof after proof of the complete authenticity of this contact with the "other side" was given. All my doubts and fears were swept aside. There are no words to adequately describe the absolute elation I felt then and continue to feel as I go through life knowing that yes, I will see my daughter in Heaven, and she knows and sees all that is happening to her earthly family.

I will not relate here the many gems that Jenny relayed to me that fully authenticated the miracle that was happening, but there is one that I will share. It is deeply personal. It is something known to absolutely no one else and dispels forever any last vestige of skepticism.

I wear a fine, gold-link chain with a small gold cross around my neck. I never remove it. It belonged to my great grandmother and I had told Nicky that one day it would belong to her. When I stood beside my daughter's casket to say my final farewell before the lid was closed, I held the cross in my hand, silently contemplating whether I should put it in Nicky's hands or whether I should continue to wear it as a symbol of our special bond. I decided to keep wearing it, but in the months that followed I often found myself wondering if I had made the right choice.

The day I visited Jenny, the cross, on its long chain, was as usual tucked well out of sight under my crew-necked tee shirt. Just as my reading was coming to an end, Jenny said, "Your daughter is showing me something in her hand. I can't quite see what it is. I'm asking her to come closer. Oh! Now I see. It's a small gold cross on a chain. Does that mean anything to you?"

By this time I was scarcely able to breathe and was at a loss for words. I fumbled at my throat and pulled the cross out from under my shirt. "Yes!" I gasped. "This cross belonged to my great-grandmother and I was going to give it to Nicky, but I didn't!"

"Oh! Yes, your daughter is smiling now, and she says, 'Tell mom it's all right about the cross!'"

So, you see, I know without any shadow of doubt that we can contact the ones we love and have lost. I still grieve for my daughter. I still miss her every day. I still long to hug her and to hear her voice. I am still moved to tears almost daily in my yearning for her physical presence. I now have the serenity of knowing I will see her again.

Thank you, thank you, thank you, Jenny, for the gift of my daughter and for the new spiritual awareness and affirmation of my Christian faith that you have given me. Bless you in your very special work.

Judy Print
28th August, 1996

I thank Judy for her strength, unconditional love and kindness, and feel privileged to share her story, which offers hope and reassurance to so many bereaved parents.

Lost at Sea

It is always a humbling experience when the spirit world directs people to see me, especially when extraordinary conditions apply. One such case was a mother and daughter, whom I met in the Los Angeles area. The year before we met, Rob and I were on a promotional book tour in California and we had stopped to give a talk in the lovely town of Paso Robles. At the time, I wondered what our real purpose was in visiting this quaint town. After meeting the two women from the Los Angeles area, the answer unfolded beautifully.

As it turns out, a woman had been passing through Paso Robles on a bus tour, and she stopped by the coffee and bookshop where I had given the talk. She purchased a copy of my book *Through the Eyes of Spirit,* and read it as she traveled. Then she sent the book to a friend who lived on Maui, one of the Hawaiian islands. The friend then forwarded the book to her mother and sister in Fullerton, California. They located me through the travel itinerary on my web page, and with a lot of geographical juggling the day arrived for me to meet mother and daughter.

I could tell from the onset both women were spiritually attuned, as they had a special glow about them. As I began to tune in, it was not long before a young man in the spirit world stepped in to communicate.

"I was a boat builder," he told me. "Please tell my mom and sister that my girlfriend and I are now safe and well."

I began to pass this information on to the two women, and they both burst into tears, embracing one another. The son went on to say, "I built the boat we were sailing on. We were sailing to your country—we were on our way to New Zealand. Our boat started to take on water in a raging storm, and we were swept overboard. The water was so cold, and we drowned very quickly." Despite all search and rescue attempts, the yacht was never to be seen again.

All this really sent shivers down my spine, as I realized that our link had been carefully orchestrated by this young man in the spirit world, who needed to reassure his family that he and his girlfriend were safe and well.

The mother and daughter told me how they now felt a strong conclusion to their feelings of never really knowing what happened. As they cried and embraced one another, they told me they felt a strong sense of closure to the ongoing nightmare of their past eight years. They also indicated that in their hearts, they could now put the son and his partner to rest. As the women were leaving, I marveled at how the spirit world had carefully planned and allowed this magical connection to take place.

A Matter of Timing

I had scheduled an appointment for a woman named Sandy, who lived thirty minutes' drive from my office. On her way to see me, she dropped her dog off to be groomed.

Sandy was in her late fifties, and had come to see me after being widowed for the second time. During her reading I discovered that both her spouses had committed suicide. Her second spouse told me in the reading that he was an alcoholic, and that Sandy found his body after he had taken his own life. He told me her exact words to him were, "You silly fool, what did you do that for?"

Another message that was distinctive in Sandy's reading was that she was going to meet up with a gentleman called Don John. Sandy said she did not recall who this man was at the time of our session.

Interestingly, on her return journey home, she was so absorbed by the information given to her from spirit that she forgot to collect her dog. As she was driving toward her hometown, she saw a large gasoline tanker in front of her and waited for a long, wide stretch of road to overtake the truck. As she passed the tanker, she caught a glimpse of the driver looking at her intently, as though he recognized her.

For the next few miles the tanker followed her, flashing his lights from time to time. He then caught up with her car, and passed her, flashing his lights and waving her over to the side of the road. Sandy eventually got the message and pulled over. As the man came toward her and placed his head inside the driver's seat window, she got a surprise, as she instantly recognized him—it was Don John, an old friend of hers. It seemed that Sandy did not recall Don's name in the reading, as she was still in a state of shock after the death of her second husband.

He was so pleased to see her, and shared with her that his spouse, also a longtime friend of Sandy's, was dying of cancer and was desperate to see her. They had lost contact with one another over the years, and Don was thrilled that they were able to exchange addresses and telephone numbers. He was also amazed at how their paths had crossed again. After that, Sandy remembered that she had left her dog behind at the groomers' and drove back to get him. I did hear that Sandy visited her friend twice before she passed over.

This was another planned sequence of events and timing that could only be instigated by the spirit world.

From South Africa to Kauai

I met Carol when she was guided by her spouse in the spirit world to travel from South Africa to the Hawaiian island of Kauai to meet me for a reading. This story begins when Carol sent me an email on August 15, 1998.

> Dear Jenny,
>
> I have finished reading your book *Through the Eyes of Spirit.*
>
> My neighbors and very good friends lent the book to me. The reason I am writing to you is that I could identify with a lot of what you have written in your book.
>
> My spouse passed away last year in February. I have experienced one vision in my dream state that was a highly positive experience. Yesterday, my plumber told me that he also had a vision of my spouse (sometime back) and that

the message he wanted the plumber to tell me
was about the existence and beauty of God!

I told this to my neighbor and that
prompted her to lend me your book. Could
you please give me some advice? Should I be
happy with this positive experience knowing
that he is happy and at peace (that was how
he came across in my vision); or should I take
this further through the help of people like
yourself?

I would appreciate it if you could respond.
Kind Regards,
          Carol

I responded to Carol's email, telling her that I felt
the plumber's comments were an accurate and positive
statement of where her spouse now resides. She asked
me why I thought it would be a plumber delivering
such a message. I explained to Carol that angels appear
in our lives in many different disguises and we call
these people "earth angels."

I believe Carol's husband spoke to the plumber as he
knew he had the correct vibration to hear him, and he
also felt that he would pass on the message to his
beloved spouse.

I offered to give Carol an absent reading from Kauai,
by tape-recording the session and posting it to her. I
also suggested that it would be more convenient to
contact a medium who lived in Johannesburg.

However, Carol, being a strong businesswoman, had
different ideas and before I knew it, she and her two

young daughters, aged two and four, were on the next flight out of Johannesburg, coming to meet me. It took them thirty-six hours of flying time to reach the garden island of Kauai. Rob and I met Carol and the girls at their hotel the next morning.

Carol was a stunning-looking woman in her mid-thirties, very petite, with beautiful solid blue eyes and blond hair, worn in a pageboy style. She wore a sleeveless black dress with pretty black shoes to match, and was wearing a gold cross around her neck. I noticed how fresh Carol looked after such a long flight, and I placed a ginger flower lei around her neck, welcoming her and the girls to the beautiful and spiritual island of Kauai.

We quickly proceeded to her room and started her reading. We both felt it was important to do this first before we got to chat and know one another. Immediately, standing next to Carol, I felt the strong presence of her husband. My entire body felt chilled and excited.

We sat down together and as I began to tune in for Carol, I felt a great surge of love almost overpower me. She had traveled such a long way and I wanted the reading to be a positive experience for her. My whole body had goose bumps on it as her spouse stepped in closely. I knew he was eager to make this communication with Carol.

He was a businessman and had a very happy disposition and personality, and this shone through brightly during our reading. I could tell he loved his wife and his girls with all his heart. He spoke of his illness with cancer, his loss of hair, and pointed to his throat area, telling me how he continued to work through his illness. He refused to take morphine or any drugs and tried alternative medicines until, sadly, it was his time to leave the earth plane. His cancer was inoperable. He spoke of his passing at work, with another colleague present.

He gave me details of their home in Johannesburg, showing me a picture of where they lived in the countryside. He told me how wonderful it was with the peacocks and animals they had on their property. He spoke of how he used to choose his wife's clothes for her, and how they loved to travel together.

I was pleased with his communication, as he told me his name was Anthony and his mother was with him in the spirit world.

Hearing her husband's name was a good piece of evidence for Carol, and as I opened my eyes and looked across at her I could see the tears rolling down her cheeks.

Most importantly, Anthony told me to tell Carol that he was at peace and that he would always love her and the girls, and would always watch over them.

During Carol's week-long stay in Kauai she was able to attend one of my workshops and meet many dear and loving souls. I believe the entire experience was healing for her and this is the letter she wrote to us after returning home to Johannesburg.

Carol's Letter

Dear Jenny & Rob,

How can we thank you for all your love and care during our visit to Kauai? You were absolutely right. Everything is in divine order and harmony. What a healing and uplifting experience. I have learned so much. I have resolved so much. I have returned exhausted but very excited about the life ahead of me and the different way I will be perceiving every aspect of it. What a beautiful gift I have been given. Thank you.

Love,

Carol

Johannesburg

Since our meeting in August 1998, Carol has had a chapel built on her property in memory of her beloved Anthony. I am sure Carol was guided to build the chapel after hearing Anthony's message about the beauty and existence of God.

Boom, Loud and Clear

The next story I found very interesting for it has once again proven to me that the spirit world really does read what we write. They can glance over our shoulders, and at times really help us to succeed with our written goals and affirmations.

The day I met Caroline for a private reading, she had been writing a letter to her loving partner in the spirit world. He had recently passed over after suffering from a long illness. Although he fought to hold onto life it was his time to leave.

One of the messages that Caroline stressed to her partner in her letter was for a clear communication from him. She scolded him in her letter for leaving, and again reiterated to him that she was expecting a strong communication from him. Apparently her partner had a great interest in walking a spiritual pathway, and Caroline felt this would help his connection with a medium.

As I sat down to tune in for her, it was only a moment before I felt a hard jolt run through my heart. I knew her partner was present, and that he had passed over with a massive heart attack. Then a very extraordinary thing happened. It was as though my mouth was opened for me and the name "Boom" came flying out. Caroline sat upright in her chair, and, with tears streaming down her face, told me it was her partner's nickname.

She also told me she had written him a letter stating that if he was able to communicate with her through a medium, and prove it was him, he would be required to use the name "Boom." This was good proof for Caroline, and Boom was soon off and away with his communication; actually it was hard to keep up with his constant chatter. I felt he was so excited with our connection, knowing that as he spoke I could hear him. He communicated very well, with many factual and important details that made Caroline very emotional. At times she did not know whether to laugh or cry!

Boom was very explicit in telling me he wanted to pass on a message to Caroline: "I want you to get on with your life, and to be happy."

He continued to say, "I am well and happy and wish you to be the same."

Boom really needed Caroline to know he was all right, and once he felt satisfied that she was convinced of this, his connection seemed to fade away. When the reading came to a conclusion, I knew that Caroline had been given the correct proof of life after death. I thanked my spirit guides for allowing Boom to make such a clear communication.

Spirit Can Hear

Just as those in the spirit world can read, they can also hear physical noises in our world. When I met Sheryl, her partner had recently passed over in a motor accident. Sheryl was in her early twenties, and had been dating her partner for approximately twelve months before his passing. They were a young couple starting out, and very much in love.

I was pleased for Sheryl that her partner, Mike, was able to come through and talk to me, letting her know he was now living in a place of glory and perfection. As I spoke to Mike in my mind, I heard an outside distraction, which sounded like a race car being revved. It was rather loud, and became annoying to me within a few moments. I was about to put my head out the window to see who was making this din when Mike whispered to me, "I really love the sound of that car, it brings joy to my heart."

For a moment I wondered why, then Mike went on to tell me he had been a race car driver. I chuckled with Sheryl as it all fell into place. He also made us laugh when he said, "We do not have telephones bothering us in the spirit world," and at that precise moment, Sheryl's cell phone rang.

Mike told me when the automobile accident had occurred, and that as he was making his transition through the veil, his last thought was of Sheryl. He was so thankful that he had experienced true love before he passed over. It was greatly reassuring for Sheryl to hear from Mike and know also that he was fully aware of her immediate surroundings. I felt sure that Mike's message would allow her to begin to pick up the pieces in her life and really start living again.

Universally United

While traveling, I get to meet many people from different countries. I always find it very exciting when working with different nationalities. During a reading, if a person does not speak English, they have an interpreter present. One woman who was living in California came to see me with her mother, Margarita, who was visiting from Mexico. She translated the reading for her mother beautifully. Margarita had many relatives in spirit, but was eager to make contact with her spouse and daughter. Her spouse stepped forward very quickly, giving her details of a ring she had recently misplaced. As he proceeded to give me information about the family to pass on, Margarita's big brown eyes widened and filled with tears.

Then her daughter in spirit stepped forward, wishing to communicate. By this time Margarita was starting to get very excited, and she chanted a little prayer as her daughter in spirit continued to communicate.

Margarita had been feeling sad about one of her sons. He had married recently, and his new spouse was not being very receptive to her. Because of this Margarita felt her relationship with her son was weakening. Her daughter in the spirit world was able to reassure her that in time her new daughter-in-law would become friendlier toward her and other family members.

I said, "I hear the name Blanca," and Margarita acknowledged this as her aunt.

Margarita said, "Oh, Blanca, Blanca, my Blanca."

It was so beautiful to see and experience this connection, particularly when a person who speaks a different language responds with such a joyful voice after receiving a message. Then a woman from spirit stepped forward, announcing herself as Luisa; with this Margarita threw her arms up in the air saying, "Momma, Momma."

It always brings joy to my heart when messages of love come from the spirit world, and are translated to those speaking foreign languages. It also brings home the message to me that we are all one in the Universe, and when a spirit wishes to communicate, they will find a way around any language barrier.

Joan's Sister

On occasion, when a spirit is eager to make a communication with a loved one, they visit me in my dreams. I feel a strong presence around me, and sometimes the spirit will speak to me, giving me their name. I will generally hear them speak to me in a voice that sounds like a whisper. The spirit will hover around me while waiting to make the vital connection with a loved one.

I recall a woman from the spirit world coming to visit me in my dream state, who identified herself as Ilene. She mentioned that I was seeing her sister Joan the next day, and said, "Joan is in a terrible state."

I could see Ilene very clearly. She was a short, plump person with dark hair and blue eyes, and looked to be in her mid-forties.

Ilene spoke to me in such a soft and serene tone; her voice sounded almost surreal and held the most wonderful vibration. She asked me to pass on a message to her sister the next day, which I happily agreed to do.

A spirit normally steps forward during a reading when a loved one is present, and very seldom do they come to visit in my sleep state. However, on occasion I have reprimanded the spirit world for disturbing my sleep, and I will say to them, "Not now please," or "wait until the morning."

Ilene went on to tell me that her sister was going through a very bad and dark time in her life. She said in her soft voice that Joan would be helped onto her pathway of light, and that she would continue to support Joan throughout her sister's lifetime. The message from Ilene came to me briefly but very strongly.

When I saw Joan the next morning, she looked like someone who had lost all purpose and focus in life. I was amazed that she had enough energy to get out of bed and get dressed. Joan was in a very bad emotional and physical state, and the light within her soul was just a flicker.

As I started to tune in for her, I once again felt the presence of her sister Ilene. The reading began quietly and slowly and was being conducted with such tender loving care. I mentioned to Joan that I had her sister Ilene communicating with me from the spirit world. Joan seemed rather shocked and surprised when I mentioned Ilene. "Are you joking?" she said, "Yes, I have a sister called Ilene in the spirit world; she passed over before I was born, and although we never met, I feel I know her well."

People can find it difficult to understand that although they have not physically met a person before they passed on, the spirit is able to see and hear them clearly from the spirit world. We may have met them previously in the spirit realms, or been linked in the dream state, and yet have no recollection of our meeting. When a spirit is genetically linked to us, they watch over us as we grow. I call these spirits our helpers.

Often a person's passing coincides with a birth—an ending and a new beginning taking place simultaneously. Ilene had passed over into the spirit world before Joan was born and had watched her grow from the spirit world.

Ilene had been assigned to Joan at birth as one of her spiritual helpers through life, and interestingly, they both knew one another but had never physically met.

We all have our guardian angels and helpers looking after us. Guardian angels and spirit guides are one and the same; religious people tend to use the name guardian angel rather than spirit guide.

Ilene's visitation reinstated the message that we should never doubt in our times of need and sadness, as we are being looked after and protected by a higher guidance that we may not even realize is there.

A Baby's Spirit Returns to the Family

For many years, I have been of the opinion that when some babies pass over into the spirit world they can reincarnate or return again to the same family very quickly. In some instances the mother may feel that she recognizes the spirit of the child she had previously lost. In a situation where the baby dies through miscarriage, premature birth, or is stillborn, the spirit of the baby often hovers around the mother for some time. This is because the baby is awaiting another opportunity to return to the family where it feels a sense of love and belonging.

I found it interesting when I received this note from Susan, an obstetrics nurse whom I had previously read for in Kauai. She had lost a baby at birth several years ago, and now believes that the same child has reincarnated back into the family through her daughter-in-law. Her new grandchild's name is Malia, and she is a miracle baby.

> Dear Jenny,
>
> I hope I can convey the emotion I felt with this story. I misplaced your tape but I do remember some of the reading you gave me on Kauai two-and-a-half to three years ago.
>
> Three items stood out in my memory of the reading. The first was that I would be worried about one of my children, and you even indicated my son and that I was not to worry, he would be all right and things would work out for him. Second, you told me I would have a granddaughter who would be very close to me, and third, that I would recognize her immediately—that she would be the spirit of the daughter I had lost at birth, prematurely.

If I have my dates right (I really should keep a journal) my son was engaged to be married at the time of the reading. Six months before his wedding date his wife-to-be was diagnosed with multiple sclerosis. Of course this was difficult, but there was never any question of their lives continuing together. They had been dating for over five years. I felt sadness, of course, as my son is very athletic, and she would not be able to keep up with him physically. To see them, though, you would recognize a strong bond of love between them. They have coped extremely well, and her family feels my son is an angel sent from God for their Veronica.

October 5th of this year my granddaughter was born out of this union. While my daughter-in-law was pregnant she went into preterm labor twice and was admitted to the hospital, where she was given steroid shots to mature the baby's lungs in case they were unable to stop the labor. Both times she was in [the] hospital, I remember "talking/praying" to the daughter I had lost, calling her by the name I had given her, Malia. I would scold her, telling her it's too early again. Not to come now; that she must wait this time. The baby did come early by four-and-a-half weeks, but because of the injections her lungs were mature and she was able to go home at 4 pounds and 12 ounces.

On the morning of the 5th of October I had called my son and told him I had finally made reservations to come later in the month.

I had been putting off making reservations because something in me told me if I made them the baby would come too soon. But on the 5th I felt safe and even if baby decided to come it would be okay, because she was old enough now. Six hours after I spoke to my son he called me from the hospital. The baby was coming. To say the least I was shocked and fortunately, because of the time difference I was able to change my reservations with no penalties to arrive the next week.

Ian, my son, of course, gave me the details over the phone of the birth. First that the baby was a girl (in my mind I thought "well Jenny was right about that") then the weight and finally the name. It was with the name where I almost dropped the phone. My first granddaughter had been named Malia Renee. My son had known, of course, that we had lost a baby girl shortly after birth but I do not ever remember telling him what I had named her.

Even though I had no recall of ever telling him the name, I still thought maybe I had mentioned it in the past, and that he subconsciously remembered. That thought was cancelled after I arrived in Albuquerque to see my granddaughter.

Ian asked me to tell his wife the story (I had told him on the phone but I wasn't sure how Veronica would take the story). Ian had told her and she thought it was wonderful and wanted me to write it down. In our conversation I found out that Ian had not named the baby. Veronica had chosen the name. While they were visiting Kauai when she was pregnant she had seen a road sign up near our house. The name of the street was Malia and she thought it was a pretty name. You can imagine my shock when I realized she had seen the same road sign I had seen when I named my daughter.

Veronica's family has a hard time with the name, being of Hispanic origin, but when it's explained it's Maria with the R replaced with an L they get it and then have no trouble remembering.

I hope you enjoyed this affirmation. It has given me a new look on life and those who watch over us.

Love and Happy Holidays
Susan

I am grateful to Susan for sharing her story. I am sure that Malia has returned to the family bringing with her healing, love, and much joy.

8

The Nightmare
of Suicide

Did you realize when you took your own life
that I would be haunted by the question
"Why?"

Did you foresee the unknowing guilt
that challenges my mind as I wrestle with
my conscience each day?

Did you realize that in gaining your
freedom you imprisoned me in tortuous
emotions?

And did you realize that the peace you
sought has brought me unrest?

Affirmations For Life
—Judith Collins

*I*n my first book I talked about what happens
to a soul after the individual has committed suicide. It is never the right decision for us to alter our
karma, as is the case when people commit suicide.
By committing suicide, the spirit has changed their
own pathway of fate, and in doing so, it will be
required to return to the earth plane many times to
work through its own karma. The soul is unable to

choose the realm where it seeks to go, but it will be guided to the realm that is most suitable for its needs at the time of passing. After suicide, the soul's life pathway is flashed in front of their eyes, showing them that they still have extensive learning and great lessons to overcome.

However, eventually every soul will find God's love and peace in the spirit world.

In some instances the tragedy of suicide can be averted when those seeking help are guided back to reality and can open lines of communication to the people in their lives with caring and loving hearts.

Statistics show that a high percentage of suicide cases occur among young people. More time, energy, understanding, and resources need to be implemented by society to help these young people through their times of depression and despair. It is worth mentioning that many of the same issues affect suicidal people of all ages, and the same prevention strategies can be used.

I recently met a woman who had lost her only son through suicide. She had presumed her son was well and happy. Just three weeks before his death, her son's best friend committed suicide. The woman felt she had not conveyed enough understanding and sympathy to her grieving son, and wondered if she could have changed her son's fate by being more sympathetic to his suffering over the loss of his friend.

Sadly, bereft parents are often left with deep feelings of guilt and regret after the suicidal death of one of their children. After the shock waves subside, there are always many unanswered questions in their minds.

In many instances the reason for the suicide remains a mystery, and a lot of the young people that leave the earth plane are loved deeply by family and friends in their daily lives. The cause of death is often not related to parental guidance or attitude.

When a young person is contemplating suicide, they generally exhibit little or no indication of how sad they are feeling, as they often continue to pretend outwardly that life is fine. In reality, however, they are quietly calculating how and when they will take their own life. Your patience will be required, as difficulties can arise when the young person isolates him- or herself by switching off from any help that is offered.

I meet many young people who feel as though they lack purpose in their lives; some feel lonely and depressed, while others feel as though they do not fit into society, and struggle to make friends. Some young people find it difficult to get work, or develop a stable relationship. There are many different situations attached to these feelings of depression; for example, they may feel unloved, rejected, humiliated, angry, or disappointed.

Many young people are sensitives, who seem easily hurt and are highly responsive to the vibrational signals sent to them from the spirit world. Often they do not know how to develop or control their intuitive gifts, leaving a void deep within their soul.

I believe that young people are searching for greater understanding of spiritual awareness; an awareness that will enlighten them toward a pathway of love, light, healing, and upliftment. Also, this new awareness will help them to focus on attracting positive activities and energy into their lives. Listening, being loving, and teaching these young individuals the art of meditation in their times of need will inevitably guide them toward a stronger spiritual pathway.

Each individual has free will in life to make their own decisions, and if the young sensitive drifts off the spiritual pathway by experimenting with excess alcohol or by taking drugs, this can hinder their judgment and lead to disastrous consequences. Experimentation with drugs and alcohol is not the route to a happy heart, as it can actually attract negative thoughts and actions toward a person.

When taking such substances, an individual does not maintain control; this action lets their emotional guard down, allowing the crown chakra area at the top of the head to open, which is our spiritual beacon of communication. After this area is opened, the vulnerable individual who indulges in drugs or alcohol can have an instant change of personality, shifting from a passive person to showing expressions of anger and violence within a very short time.

Dark entities that come from the lower astral plane hover around, waiting to enjoy the intoxicated or drug-related feelings of the individual, and they can enter a physical body very quickly, taking over their personality. These entities are spirits that have passed over who are not evolved souls. They would have chosen not to walk in the light when living on the earth plane, and after death they have not reached the higher astral conscious planes. Instead, they hover around the lower planes, waiting to see the light so they can be helped over to the first plane of consciousness.

When these entities are around, the young person may hear a voice in their mind, telling them to take their own life. Although this is the voice of the entity, it sounds and is very real. In these situations many people are diagnosed as schizophrenics, but I believe they are psychic people out of control. They can hear clairaudiently; unfortunately, they do not have an understanding of metaphysics and the supernatural, or how to protect themselves.

In one instance I read for a young woman who had recently lost her brother to suicide. According to the woman, she felt her brother was a happy person. One day, after he had been drinking, he told her that he was going downstairs to get his wallet from his truck. He reached under the seat, and next to his wallet was a gun he carried for protection, as his truck's route was based in a higher crime area of the United States. Instead of retrieving his wallet, however, he picked up the gun, put it to his head, and shot himself. His sister found him dead within a few moments.

Before a person contemplates suicide, they may be experiencing a deep, dark time in their life. These dark

es are often given to test one's faith, and these tests
e been chosen by us prior to our return to the earth
plane from a previous lifetime.

Buddhists welcome painful tests and challenges in
life; they believe that working through our burdens
helps each individual to grow spiritually. When these
challenges are overcome, knowledge and strength is
gained from the self-chosen lessons and experiences.
Once we evaluate our lessons and learn from them, life
will then begin to feel happier again by restoring a sense
of upliftment, achievement, and contentment.

During times of despair, it can enhance your faith in
God to pray, and your prayers can be practiced from
the realms of your heart. The power of prayer enables
you to trust in your inner guidance and brings about a
feeling of inner peace that emanates from deep within
your heart, healing the depths of despair and erasing
feelings of depression that are festering within an individual's soul.

Once a young person is guided to their true purpose
in life, their life will then move ahead in leaps and
bounds. One of the greatest pleasures in life can be
attained by serving humanity as a volunteer, or working
for an organization that specializes in helping others.

Stepping onto the pathway of serving humanity
brings many gifts from the spirit world that are offered
to us in different forms. For example, you may be
introduced to a wonderful partner or friend, find a new
occupation or home, gain more wisdom and spiritual

understanding, or be given love and an inner peace that is indescribable.

I advise that you enlist the help of either a doctor, psychologist, spiritual counselor, naturopath, or healer to offer aid to a suicidal person. Try to turn every stone to be of assistance to those who cannot see the light at the end of the tunnel, and remember to "let go and let God." Having a depressed person living with you is among one of the hardest lessons in life; both natural and orthodox medicine can be highly beneficial in uplifting a person's emotional state of mind.

The following stories are about people who took their own lives. In each case, they could not have been more loved, respected, or supported by their families.

Stephanie

When Stephanie came to see me, she and her spouse, Brian, had lost their son Colin to suicide. Colin was working through some problems with a friend prior to his passing, and was feeling very upset and confused. The police had arrested Colin over a minor detail, locking him up in a police station holding cell. Knowing that Colin was very depressed, his family pleaded with the police to let their son come home.

Colin had telephoned Stephanie in a distressed state of mind prior to the arrest, and the family feared for his safety. However, attempts to get the police to listen and understand the seriousness of the situation were totally ignored. As the family pleaded with police, Colin was attempting to take his own life. The police found him moments later, but he died in the hospital's intensive care unit five days after the event.

I didn't know any of this when I began the reading for Colin's mother, but as I started to pray and tune in for her, I was overwhelmed by her son's feelings of deep love and affection for her.

I commenced the reading:

"I feel the spirit of a young man standing behind you, Stephanie."

"Yes."

"Do you have a son in the spirit world?"

"Yes."

"I feel short of breath. It feels as though he has something around his neck."

"Yes."

"I feel confusion around your son. Did he pass as a result of an accident?"

"No, not really, he committed suicide. He hung himself in a police cell."

"Oh my Lord! Because of his confused state before he passed over, our communication is a little difficult. I shall try to work harder and see if your son is ready for me to bring in a clearer connection.

"He is stepping in closer now, and talking about the police who were on duty the night he was arrested. Your son is telling me that he feels very remorseful about taking his own life and the pain he has put the family through."

As I listened carefully I wanted to make sure I was hearing and translating the details from Colin correctly. I was also seeking proof of his connection to give to his mother.

"I can see two older ladies standing with your son; one of them is your mother."

"Yes."

"She tells me that she had trouble with her circulation when she was alive, and thanks you for helping her. She also tells me that you are a nurse—is this correct?"

"Yes."

"Your mother is showing me a photo in a family album of her twin brother and sister. She's laughing at the resemblance between her sister and your new granddaughter."

"Yes," Stephanie responded immediately.

"Your mother is also saying, Please tell Stephanie we have Gordon with us in the spirit world."

Stephanie let out a big gasp.

"Oh, yes. Gordon is my brother who passed over at an early age."

"Also, your mother is saying, I keep a watchful eye on your father. He is still handsome, and I see that he continues to wear his favorite green cardigan. I will come to get him, when it is his time to leave the earth plane."

Stephanie laughed out loud, and said, "Dad always loves wearing his green cardie, and I know he misses Mom tremendously."

I felt as though the reading was starting to flow as the vibrational energy in the room was increasing.

"Colin tells me that there was a passing in your family close to a birth."

"Yes."

I asked Stephanie to wait a moment as I clarified this message.

Colin continued, "It was my passing close to the birth of my niece."

Stephanie's eyes filled with tears as she acknowledged that Colin's sister gave birth the day of her brother's funeral service. The baby was born at 7:00 A.M., and Colin's funeral service was at 1:00 P.M. After giving birth, Colin's sister was able to attend her brother's funeral.

This message really took my breath away, and reiterates that in some instances the timing of a passing and a birth in the same family can occur very close together. After hearing this message I felt Stephanie and Brian's new granddaughter had arrived to bring tremendous love and healing to the family. It seemed almost imperative that the spirit world had sent this wee angel to the family for this purpose.

In situations of extreme sadness I have to hold back my own emotions, as I can feel the unsurmountable pain around a person and the spirit at the same time. If I wept openly with them, it would weaken the vital connection to their loved ones in the spirit world. I need to step back emotionally from the situation, so that I can continue to hear the spirit and pass on messages of love and support to my clients.

As the communication continued, Colin stepped in close again, and I could see him rubbing his nose.

"Your son is rubbing the right side of his nose, pointing to a scar."

"Yes, he had a scar caused from a car accident."

"He is telling me that he knows about his father's band, and that his Dad is trying to get in touch with old band members that he played with over thirty years ago."

"Yes, this is very true."

"Please also tell Dad that I often visit him while he is playing the electronic organ.

"I used to love sitting with him under the large weeping elm tree on the river bank, overlooking the stream that runs through our property."

"Yes, they loved spending time together."

Colin announced, "I help Dad in his workshop. I pop in and visit him from time to time to watch him work on airplanes. I know he feels my presence in the workshop."

"Yes, his father is an engineer who works on airplanes."

"Colin is also telling me that he likes the alterations you have made to your home, and says the house sparkles when seen from above."

Just then a woman stepped forward in spirit and announced herself as Helen, telling me that she was Colin's great-grandmother.

Stephanie acknowledged, "Yes, Helen is my husband's grandmother."

She wished to tell the family that all was well in the spirit world.

Colin stepped back in, "Please also tell my brother that I am thrilled with the song he has written and recorded for me. I want to send my love and gratitude to him."

(I find that when people have such deep tragedies in their lives they are often guided and inspired to write songs and poetry.)

I could tell that Colin was a very spiritual and sensitive young man, and that he was trying so hard to reassure his mother and family that he was now at peace in the spirit world. As my link with Colin started to weaken, he sent his eternal love to his Mom, Dad, and family. Because mother and son had such a strong love link, this made my job of communicating with him a little easier.

As Stephanie walked toward the door, she let out a deep sigh of relief. I felt she could continue to bask in the love that her son was showering upon her.

A few months after having the privilege of reading for Stephanie, she sent me a copy of the song that their son David had written as a tribute to his brother in the spirit world. She enclosed a short letter that said:

Thank you, Jenny, for your loving nature and the reassurance you give to so many people in distress. Good luck with your new book. I am sure many people will be blessed by reading it.

The reading you did for me was also a great help to our family after the tragic death of our son Colin. Suicide leaves so many unanswered questions in the minds of those left behind.

It is reassuring to know that life does in fact go on after death, and that one day we will meet again.

Bless you,
Stephanie

Louise

After making a heart-wrenching connection with the spirit world, I can be left feeling drained. Following my session with Stephanie, I was scheduled to see a woman named Louise, who had sounded rather distressed when I spoke with her on the telephone. Although I was tired, I felt there was an urgent need for Louise to make contact with the spirit world.

Louise was in her mid-fifties, and her beautiful face was warm and loving. She had big blue eyes that seemed to hold a deep well of sadness. Louise was showing the strain of her only daughter committing suicide. Jane had been twenty-four years old at the time of her death, and had left behind two young children: an eight-month-old daughter and an eighteen-month-old son. The children were now being raised by Louise.

But I was to find out in Louise's reading that Jane's death had been only the beginning of her tragedies.

At the time of Jane's death, Louise and her thirteen-year-old son Joe were crew members on a sailboat, sailing in English waters. Typically when Louise was sailing she would wake at sunrise and read for a while. One morning she awoke surprised to see a vision of her daughter, who was living in New Zealand at the time. Louise was startled to see a clear vision of Jane with her long fair hair flowing over her shoulders. Three days after seeing the apparition of her daughter, Interpol made contact with Louise, handing her a note with the sad news of her daughter's passing.

I discovered in Louise's reading that her son Joe had also died, and sitting beside him in the spirit world was a black Labrador dog. Apparently the dog was shot outside Louise's home, and two days after the dog was mysteriously killed, the home burned to the ground.

It made me shudder to think of all the pain and heartache Louise has had to endure. On the night of the fire she heard her son go out. Later she was awakened by an electrical fire in their home, but she managed to escape with her two grandchildren.

After her reading, Louise told me that as she and her grandchildren stood together in their nightclothes and helplessly watched the fire burn with a blazing fury, it did not matter about her house or material possessions, all she cared about was the safety of her children. She did not know yet that her son Joe had returned home that evening, and that he was actually in the burning house. Firefighters tried desperately to enter the house and rescue him, but it was too late to save him. Had her dog been alive prior to the fire, he perhaps would have alerted the family with his barking.

In Louise's reading, her son whispered his first name to me as Joe Russell. When he was on the earth plane, Joe Russell always told his mom that he did not think he would live to be twenty-five years of age. He told me how his grandfather, John Alfred, came to meet him and take him over to the other side. Joe was so happy to tell me that his Mom had a lovely photo of him taken at a wedding just two days before he passed. Also, Louise's birth mother was present in the spirit world; even though Louise had been adopted when she was seven months old, she felt she knew and could remember her birth mother.

Louise's daughter Jane also stepped forward and told me that Peter was with them in the spirit world. Louise put her hands over her mouth and said that Peter was her sister's son, who went over as a young child. I told her I could see a white bird—it looked like a dove— flying around her children in spirit, and Louise said that she always wanted a white bird. Perhaps this was a dove of peace being sent to her from the spirit world.

Jane went on to tell me that she and her brother had different fathers; that her dad was in Australia.

She told me, "My dad needs a good shake-up."

Louise acknowledged that she felt Jane's father had played a major part in her daughter's problems.

Jane said, "I am so pleased at how Mom is raising my children. She is a nurse, you know."

Then Jane whispered, "My mom is just so precious, and I am so happy to be here in spirit with my brother Joe. Please tell Mom, I have felt so remorseful about leaving her with the burden of raising my children, but I just could not cope any more."

I asked Jane how she took her life, but she did not want to discuss the details. I can never extract information from those in spirit; they must offer the information freely, and this will only happen when they are ready to do so.

Because Louise was such a spiritual person, and receptive to messages from her loved ones in the spirit world, I knew that she would not have any difficulty having her own conversations with her children. I felt she had the ability to make contact with them both, and felt that Jane would never be too far away as she still watches over and links very closely to her children.

Louise tells people that she gained so much strength and wisdom through her traumas. Both her children have been taken from her, and now she is raising her two grandchildren. She tells people that it is all right to weep freely, and she often strokes Jane's hair in her photographs. I know that a big part of Louise's heart has been taken from her, and that she will never fully recover from the trauma of losing both her children.

It takes so much courage to walk forward in life the way Louise has, and I am in awe of her strength and positive attitude. She will help many others through their times of grief and pain, and I am sure the spirit world continues to give her love, healing, upliftment, and strength to conquer each day. She has never lost her faith throughout her years of sadness. God bless her always in her work of showing other people that even through the deepest heartaches, we must still continue to live and forge ahead in life.

Donna

I often sense overwhelming feelings when waiting to see a client. I start to feel anxious before my client arrives, and when this happens, I know the spirit is eager to make contact. This happened to me when I saw Donna on January 6, 1998. As she walked through the door, I was immediately struck by the grief cloud above her head.

Her appointment was scheduled at 10:00 A.M., and in the early hours of the same morning, the police had awakened Donna to tell her that her uncle had committed suicide.

Donna was very close to her uncle; he was like a father figure to her and he lived next door to her house. Miraculously, as her uncle's body lay in the mortuary, he was able to communicate some details to her during my reading. First I discovered that he had shot himself through the heart.

Her uncle had read my first book, and knew that it was wrong to alter his karma. He had discussed this with Donna often, and after she heard the news of her uncle's passing, she turned her house upside down to find her copy of *Through the Eyes of Spirit*, to reread the chapter on suicide.

Although Donna's uncle struggled to communicate at first, he mentioned that he had been divorced twice, and spoke of Donna's children, his grandniece and grandnephew.

During Donna's reading her uncle showed me several beautiful red roses he wished to pass on to her.

I could see a priest standing next to Donna's uncle in the spirit world; she told me her uncle used to speak to her extensively about spiritualism and religion. The priest standing next to his soul was dressed in a long gold coat and wore a pyramid-shaped hat. I felt that the uncle had reached a place in the higher realms where healing, peace, and happiness would now engulf him. It was a blessing for Donna to hear from her uncle so soon, particularly under such tragic circumstances.

After Donna's reading, I received the following letter.

> Jenny,
> The reading you did for me last week has come to have so much significance for my Mom and myself. It has been a source of comfort and the beginning of understanding and acceptance following my uncle's death.
> The red roses he gave out during the reading have come up again and again since.

Both Mom and I have drawn a lot of strength from the reading and my sister has yet to hear the tape, but we have told her a lot about it.

Our family was amazed at the time gap between his passing over and my scheduled appointment with you; it was only a matter of a few hours.

It was also very special that my granddad came through too.

Thank you from the bottom of my heart.
Donna

Kirsten

I saw Kirsten after her fiancé, James, committed suicide. Unless I record details after a reading, I seldom recall the information that has been given to a person from the spirit world. I did, however, receive a card from Kirsten after her reading, and I loved the way she described where her fiancé now is.

Dear Jenny,

Thank you, thank you, thank you for my reading, and words could never express my gratitude or the amount of peace that I now have knowing that my darling James is okay and happy and free.

Yesterday, it was four months since James left us. I took him some beautiful red roses. I just lay them down on his grave and then lay myself down next to his grave on the soft grass and tasted his peace and love, without regret or guilt. I felt the pure love and deep sadness in my heart and it was magical.

I played the tape of the reading to James' Mom, Margaret, and she was able to verify some of the information I did not know about. You told me about a John in the spirit world; this is Margaret's father. Also Robert was James' grandfather and greatgrandfather. The motorcycle you saw is in James' little brother's room, which James had when he was very small.

Yesterday, I purchased a beautiful bright-lemon-colored sweatshirt. The color yellow was following me around everywhere I looked, and really standing out in my vision until I got the sweatshirt, and it felt good as soon as I put it on next to my skin.

It feels like a warm little lightbulb has gone on in my heart.

I feel myself as though James never really left us, and that he is always with me in my heart. I have asked James if he would teach me to surf when I get to spirit in seventy years.

My grandmother is in the spirit world also, and she loves baking. I am going to ask her to bake James a cake in August for his birthday. I think they would both like that.

Thank you again, Jenny.

Blessings, love, and white light for you.

Kirsten

Although it is important to express and process your grief after the loss of a loved one to suicide, never hesitate to express your joy and happiness at memories or events that bring your loved one to mind. The departed souls will start to heal so much faster when they can hear our joy and laughter again. It is the vibration of laughter that draws them in to make a closer connection with their loved ones.

9

Hilarious Moments

With a kind of relaxed shiver I fell off to
sleep, with only the sound of silence. Then
somewhere behind the building I heard pigs
snorting.

Out on a Limb
—Shirley MacLaine

A medium's work is never dull, and each day seems to be interspersed with sadness and hilarious moments. Fortunately, those in the spirit world do have a sense of humor and often bring laughter into my work, providing upliftment for both my client and me.

Mabel

I met Mabel when she drove her mother and sister-in-law to a spiritual gathering that was held at our friends' home in Wrightwood, California.

Mabel was wearing shorts, a T-shirt, and men's work boots; her hair was pulled back in a ponytail. She was in her mid-forties, and her large, black-rimmed glasses and cap seemed to cover most of her face. When we were introduced, I could tell that she was a kind-hearted person, and seemed to have a nurturing quality about her.

I noticed during the evening that Mabel looked a little somber and seemed uncertain about the group's authenticity and communication with the spirit world. As the meeting was drawing to an end, I asked the group to tune in and give one person a message. I was fascinated to watch all the group members train their eyes on Mabel and begin to tune into the spirit world for her.

What happened next may have convinced Mabel of life-after-death. One of the group members said she could see tuna fish and frogs' legs around Mabel. Everyone laughed, but to our surprise, Mabel suddenly burst into tears. She would explain later. Another woman in the group said she could see a picture of Red Skelton around Mabel. By this time Mabel had her head in her hands. Apparently she was not prepared for the next message, and seemed amazed when another member of the group said a gentleman named Bob was standing behind her.

Mabel stopped crying after about ten minutes, and told the group that she had thought at the beginning of the evening that the afterlife was a load of rubbish. She had only come that night because she was the driver. But, she told us, prior to the meeting she had silently prayed that if her father, Bob, was alive and well in another dimension, then he would need to bring her indisputable proof of this. And so he had as it transpired, when Mabel was a young girl she and her father would catch and cook frogs' legs and eat them with tuna fish while watching the Red Skelton show on television.

For the group, the evening's revelation reinforced the message that we should not analyze or edit information given to us from the spirit world, as sometimes simple and unusual messages may be of the most importance to the recipient. In Mabel's situation, we had all chuckled to ourselves over the unusual messages given to her, and I was so proud of the group for passing them on exactly as they were received. Mabel's messages obviously had a profound affect on her, and as she walked away that evening we could all see the look of peace and contentment on her face.

John's Alien Experience

They say a medium can never be certain about who comes to their door, and this rang true for me when three strange men came to my door one evening several years ago. Although I did not think the experience was funny at the time, I can now laugh about it.

I had been busy with clients on that particular day, and at five o'clock, three men who did not have an appointment knocked at my door.

Two of the men were short and very slimly built, while the third man was over six feet tall, with a large upper torso. The tall man was wearing an army T-shirt and the muscles in his arms looked like watermelons. The men seemed desperate to talk and asked me if they could come in. They told me that their tall friend, John, was in the army, and he had discovered some "top secret" information that he was afraid to share with them. They pleaded with me to talk with John in private, and stressed it was urgent that he share his story with a psychic medium.

I ushered the two small men into our living room and asked them to wait there. A strange chilling feeling overcame me as I walked down the passage with John, taking him to the special room I use for readings.

I began to tune in and picked up an unusual energy surrounding John. Although he looked unwell and his face was pale and serious, his physical appearance looked strong in his T-shirt, as he sat glaring at me with his arms folded. Again a weird feeling overcame me as I proceeded to tune in for him. I suddenly felt darkness around John, and questioned in my mind the hidden agenda for this visit.

John leaned toward me asking me if I believed in UFOs and aliens.

"Yes," I replied. "Indisputably there has been interesting documentation about spaceships, aliens, and the like." However, I pondered to myself that I did not feel like entering into this conversation with him at the time.

John leaned forward again, this time even closer to me, and said in a deep, husky voice, "Good, I am glad you believe in aliens, because this is why I am here." He told me that he had seen the film *Alien* and that he himself had an alien living in his physical body, except it was not spelled "alien," this alien was actually spelled "alein." He pronounced each letter for me two or three times.

I looked at John's face, and his expression led me to believe he was very serious. His conversation was starting to make me feel rather uncomfortable. In a sense it frightened me, and I knew I must also be very careful and sensitive in the way I handled the situation.

John leaned forward once again and this time in an aggressive voice said, "I have come here today for you to remove this 'alein' from me by performing psychic surgery."

This really sent shivers down my spine and I knew I had to get John out of the room quickly.

Many people may have heard or read about psychic surgeons, particularly in the Philippines, where psychic surgeons and spiritual healers have had some amazing results in curing people of very serious illnesses. Some of the successes in the Philippines have been filmed and carefully documented. However, my job as a medium did not fit into the category of removing an alien from a person who had recently watched a movie and was totally convinced that an alien had entered his physical body. I also did not consider myself qualified to perform an exorcism on him, although my silent prayers were being directed at him.

I looked at John and knew I must get him out of the room, as I felt unsafe being alone with him. With a serious expression, I looked across at him and said, "Oh, I see, I am sure we can help you. Now just relax and take a few deep breaths. But, I must speak with your friends waiting in the living room, so please come with me."

Luckily, John seemed to follow my instructions, and he got up and followed me down the passageway. I felt uncomfortable with him because he was very quickly becoming aggressive. We walked into the lounge where his friends, whom I later named Tom and Jerry, were waiting, and I asked who was in charge. The shorter of the two men stepped forward, and as I looked at them both, I knew that they might not have been very helpful had I needed to call upon them in any aggressive situation.

"Well," I said to the man in charge, "your friend has a problem and needs some help. I am unable to assist him and feel that he needs to seek advice from a professional person at the hospital."

I was trying to be diplomatic and suggest that perhaps John needed psychiatric treatment. I told them that there are qualified people who have the expertise to deal with John's situation. The short man stared at me as I suggested that he take his friend up to ward 17 at the local hospital, which is the psychiatric ward.

He looked at me starry-eyed and said, "Oh, we have just come from there. No one could help us."

This took my breath away and I replied, "Well, you are going back there, and I will phone the hospital now to let them know that you are returning."

He smiled at me and told me that all three of them had been patients in the psychiatric ward, and that is how they knew they must contact a psychic medium.

As we said goodbye in a friendly manner and I ushered the three men out of the house, I prayed that they would receive the correct help they needed. I then phoned the hospital to explain that John needed to have a consultation with a medical person. I must confess that for a short time I did feel threatened by John; fortunately, I always feel an enormous light of protection surrounding me. The men were harmless in a sense, but a situation of this type could become serious if not handled correctly.

There are some mediums who can deal more adequately than I with psychiatric patients, and many of them are very helpful to such people. As I have already mentioned, I think that many people who are diagnosed as schizophrenics do possess psychic powers, but this energy placement is unprotected and out of control. The schizophrenic person hears voices in their head, telling them to do all sorts of weird and wonderful things. The voice they hear is from a mischievous spirit who resides in the lower astral realms. These spirits are not evolved, and are on the lookout for an individual who is vulnerable and does not have control of their psychic gift. This is why you will often hear a schizophrenic person telling you that they heard a voice giving them instructions. The voice is very real, but sadly the messages given to the schizophrenic person can be damaging—for example, telling them to break windows or be destructive in a way that could be harmful to themselves and others.

I knew in my heart that John and his friends would be all right, and I also considered that when John was in my presence, the spirit world had silently helped to clear away some of the mental blocks he held toward the vision of his alien visitor. It makes me smile even now when I think about the excited look on John's friend's face as he told me that they had all just come from the psychiatric unit.

Psychometry in the Street

Many years ago, when I accompanied my husband Robert to Auckland on a business trip, I had an interesting experience with psychometry. Psychometry is being able to read an object, be it a letter, jewelry, photos, houses, rocks, trees, and so on from its vibrations.

In Auckland, we booked into a nice hotel overlooking some rose gardens and it was all very pleasant. Rob went off to his business meetings each day, and I filled in my time browsing around the shops. I recall waking up one morning and saying to my spirit guides that I felt a bit lonely with no one to talk to and no spiritual work or soul food to nourish me. I asked them if they could show me something spiritual to give me some soul food this day. It wasn't long before my guides delivered my soul food. As I walked toward the nearest shopping center, a large bus full of women in their sixties, who appeared to be on a bowling tour, pulled up alongside me.

As three of the women stepped from the bus, I heard one of them say, "Oh, look over there! That sign says 'tarot card readings upstairs.' Let's go and explore."

With that, I looked over at the sign, which I had not noticed during the past week, although I must have walked past it at least a dozen times. As the ladies proceeded up the stairs to visit the tarot reader, I could not resist going to look myself. As the four of us neared the top of the stairs, we saw the tarot card reader's sign, which indicated that she had stepped out for an hour. Her sign advertised half-hour readings at an exorbitant fee. The three women gathered together and remarked to themselves how disappointed they were that she was out, although they thought her fee was unacceptable.

At this point, I felt the women hadn't even noticed me standing beside them. I don't know what came over me when I casually remarked, "Oh, what a pity, I do not have my tarot cards with me."

With that remark, all three heads seemed to turn simultaneously and they all looked at me intently.

"Do you read the cards?" they asked.

"Yes," I replied. "I read them intuitively."

"Where do you live?" they asked.

I explained that I was on holiday and that we were staying in a hotel nearby.

"Oh, what a pity," they said. "We have only got an hour and then we must catch our bus again."

One of the ladies seemed insistent and almost desperate for a message.

She asked me, "Isn't there something else you could do for us?"

I felt excited as they gathered around me. "Yes," I said, "would you like me to do some psychometry for you?"

"Yes, please," they quickly replied, and then asked me what psychometry was. One of the ladies suggested we get going, as time was moving on.

"Where shall we do it?" I asked, as we walked back down the stairs together.

We looked for a place to sit, and since we could not see a place that was suitable, ended up on a concrete wall paralleling the street. I still smile when I think about it. There I was, sitting on the wall with the three ladies lined up beside me, each with a piece of jewelry in hand, awaiting their turn.

I gave the first lady her mini-reading, and she seemed very pleased. Then it was the second lady's turn. By this time some of their friends from the bus had gathered around, and it felt like a psychic fair was developing. I had visions of myself wearing large gold earrings and a gypsy scarf around my head. I had always been told by one of my main spiritual teachers, Elma Farmer, that a good medium should be able to tune in anywhere; it would not matter whether you were sitting in the middle of Piccadilly Circus, or asked on the spur of the moment, you ought to be able to switch in to spirit in any situation and read for a person.

After I had completed the pyschometry readings for the three ladies, they were all smiling and seemed happy with the information given to them. One of the ladies, who seemed the most desperate, received a message that she had been waiting to hear for some time, and this pleased us both greatly. I knew the spirit world had orchestrated our meeting as I had walked past their bus right on cue.

Then one of the ladies stepped forward and asked me how much she owed me. I blushed and felt embarrassed; this was good fun for me and I had not intended taking any money from them. To be perfectly honest, I had never thought about money throughout our time together. After all, I had found them, in a sense.

"No, thank you," I said to her. "It has been such a great pleasure meeting you all."

"Oh, we insist," she said. "We are so pleased to meet you. Please take a small donation from us."

Two of the ladies handed me a crisp twenty-dollar bill. Again I said that I could not take their money, but they insisted. We hugged one another and they walked away smiling.

I skipped back to my hotel, grinning, and thanked the spirit world for such an enlightening day. That evening, when Rob returned home from his busy schedule of meetings, he asked me what I had done during the day.

"Oh," I replied, "not much. I went out and browsed around the shops."

"Didn't you have anything exciting happen to you today?" he asked.

"Oh yes," I casually remarked. "I did. That's right. I made forty dollars in the street today!"

For a moment, Rob's face registered a teensy bit of shock as he processed this puzzling news. I went on to explain my encounter with the three ladies and how I gave them psychometry readings in the street.

Rob laughed heartily as he said, "Jen, you really had me worried there for a minute."

I had not wanted monetary reward that day, but soul food, and I felt my prayers had been answered. Even now, recalling the encounter with the three ladies and my street side psychometry readings, always brings a smile to my face.

The Dog That Got Away

While writing my first book, *Through the Eyes of Spirit,* on the island of Kauai, Rob and I were invited to stay in our friends beachfront home for two weeks while they traveled to Las Vegas for a vacation. We jumped at the chance, but there was only one problem: our friends' eldest daughter had a three-month-old male puppy. After meeting this cute, wee puppy, we were apprehensive about staying in the house. The pup was happy to bite and chew everything in sight, and like all babies, needed constant supervision. We were also concerned because the property was not fenced and was close to a busy road. It seemed unfair to tie the puppy up. However, we were afraid that he would run away if he wasn't restrained.

The offer to stay in their lovely home was tempting, as it would be a good place to continue my writing, but we were dubious about taking on the responsibility of the puppy. However, just one day before we were to move into the house, the puppy ran away.

The family was devastated, and Rob and I reassured them that our intuition told us the pup was fine and would be returned back to them safe and sound. The next day, they left for their vacation and we told them that we would advertise for their lost dog in the local paper.

After they left, Rob and I looked at one another and grinned. I asked him, "Are you thinking what I'm thinking, that the spirit world has sent the puppy away for two weeks so that I can concentrate on writing?"

We both felt sure it would return within a short time of our leaving and that in the meantime, it would be found and well cared for. During our stay in the house, we did receive a couple of concerned phone calls from the family, asking about the puppy, and each time we reassured them that we trusted the puppy would be returned safe and well.

Our glorious two-week stay in the house ended, and we headed back to the house we had been renting. Within an hour of leaving our friends' house, they called to inform us that a woman had phoned saying she had seen the advertisement in the paper, and had found the puppy and cared for it the past two weeks. The puppy was returned that afternoon, wagging its tail and none the worse for its little adventure and holiday. Rob and I laughed for days afterward. Although we had little doubt of the pup's safety, we were pleased he was well and had been in good hands.

We knew the spirit world was helping with the special project of writing a book, and during the two weeks at the beach house I finished the manuscript. We felt so blessed that divine intervention played such an important role as we once again experienced the spirit of love.

10

What Does It Mean, Jenny?

Everyone is forgiven because no one is more
spiritual than anyone else.
    Everyone is equal.

Change We Must
—Nana Veary

*T*o satisfy their great curiosity on these top-
ics, people often ask me about my work as a
medium and about the life hereafter. I want to share
some of these questions and my answers about how
I perceive communications from the spirit world, in
the form of an interview conducted by my husband
and partner, Robert.

Q: What does being clairvoyant and clairaudient
mean?

A: Clairvoyance means that the medium can see
a spirit clearly. The spirit(s) usually manifest themselves to the medium as they appeared when living

on earth. For example, if the spirit was wearing hospital pajamas or a suit when they passed over, in my experience this is how they will show themselves to me, as if in a clear color photograph. Often they point out how tall they were or that they had a deep scar on their chin.

Clairaudience is when the medium hears the spirit. The voice is an impression which flashes across my mind, like a typewritten subliminal message. I can tell whether the spirit has an accent or not, and whether they were softly spoken or loud when living. If the spirit keeps clearing their throat to communicate, you can almost guarantee this is how I will hear them, and very likely I will take on this action myself while delivering a message to my client.

When people pass over they take their personalities with them, so be prepared: if a person was grumpy, loud, or angry on earth, then this is usually how the spirit will appear to the medium.

Q: Do you really hear the spirits giving you their names in a reading?

A: Yes, I often hear key names in a reading. Sometimes the spirit will identify themselves immediately, and other times they will whisper their name to me in the last few moments of a reading. Be reassured, if a spirit wishes me to hear their name, then there is no stopping them.

I read for a lady whose husband in spirit could not get me to hear his name, so he showed me a picture of Donald Duck, and of course his name was Donald.

The spirit can be very clever and funny at the same time, and have clever methods of gaining my attention. On another occasion I was reading for a lady who had recently lost her husband. The spirit kept gesturing toward my neck. I could not understand why he kept saying, "Neck, neck." I asked his wife if she had problems with her neck, and she replied "No." After a few moments I realized that he was trying to say his name, Neck, and of course it was Nick; I finally heard him. His wife was delighted at his persistence to bring his name through.

Q: Do you believe that people receive healing when seeking out a medium?

A: Yes, I believe that God has directed them to us for a reading. During this time, the spirit world can attempt to channel a great deal of healing energy through the medium. Often, a lot of cleansing takes place for the client as well. Through the spoken word and presence of the medium they can experience the God love that is being channeled through to them.

A client may shed tears during this cleansing time, feeling a great sense of relief that a weight has been lifted from their shoulders. I have had clients tell me that they felt as though a warm hand had been placed on their heart chakra area, and from this experience they felt as though they had received spiritual healing.

Not only the departed spirit but also the spirit guides and guardian angels, along with the loving stream of God energy of the individual who is coming for the reading are working together to send, communicate, and pour information and healing through the medium on many levels at once. Not all of these are verbal, although the energy or vibratory quality of the medium's voice may be used to convey or transmit or bring a strong stream of healing or uplifting energy into the room.

The medium's life force emanating from his or her aura and chakras, especially the solar plexus and third eye areas, will be amplified with the help of spirit. In other words, much healing can take place, not only through the words spoken but throughout the entire experience. Spirit takes the opportunity to send through as much love, forgiveness, reassurance, and other uplifting qualities as possible, and sometimes this has an effect in terms of physical healing as well in the weeks and months ahead.

Q: How does the spirit know to visit the medium in the presence of a client?

A: Prior to a client visiting a medium, those in the spirit world have often orchestrated the meeting by visiting clients in their sleep state and implanting the idea to seek out a medium for this type of communication.

The medium has worked for many years to lift his or her God consciousness and this vibration creates a beacon of light for the spirit to connect with. It is possible for a person to develop such a beacon of light with intuition and devotion to God—many people are filled with light that they themselves do not realize.

Nonetheless, even with the help of the medium, the spirit will not come forth unless they are ready, and of course they only come because their loved one is present with the medium. The medium does not have the ability to call a spirit up at will. We cannot dial up Elvis Presley or Princess Diana and ask how they're doing. We must wait for the spirit to come forth when they are ready. It is a joint orchestration between the medium's spiritual guides, the client's spiritual guides, and the spirit the client wishes to contact that enables the connection between spirit and client to take place.

Q: Can you tell me a bit more about our spiritual guides?

A: It takes years and years for mediums to know the true identity of their spiritual guides. Our spiritual guides are evolved souls in the spirit world who are assigned to us at birth, to silently teach us and guide us through life. Some people refer to spirit guides as their guardian angels. We have one main guide who walks through life with us. I know my main spiritual guide's name is Amos; he speaks to me, and I feel his presence and love around me constantly. We also have spiritual helpers who assist and comfort us through life. Often our helpers are our own loved ones who have already passed over into the spirit world and have a strong desire to help us.

Q: When a person passes over and they have had a strong love link with a person on earth, does the spirit hover around the person on earth or do they come forward only in the presence of a medium?

A: The spirit often visits in times of need in the dream state, and through our loving thoughts we can call them in to be near us. In fact, most people have no idea how much company and help they receive from the spirit world on an ongoing basis. We can often link with a loved one in our sleep state after their passing. Sometimes they visit us in the dream state on an anniversary or birthday or special occasion. The client will awaken the next morning recalling the dream or visitation from their loved ones, feeling the embrace of love and comfort that has been showered upon them. Alternatively, sometimes the spirit is busy; for example, we are all assigned jobs in the spirit world, from gardening to doctoring. Our jobs are designated and determined before we pass over; it is as though the spiritual council decides. All our deeds on earth are recorded in the gigantic spiritual computers sometimes called the Akashic records. If we do a good job on earth, then it is likely that we will continue to be in a place of enjoyment, sharing the talents we once possessed on earth in the spirit world. We go to a plane of consciousness and activity that aligns with the inner level of consciousness and refinement of character that we have attained on earth.

Sometimes if a spirit is confused prior to passing, then the medium may pick up that the spirit is still hovering around a loved one on earth. Recently I helped a man who had passed over with a brain tumor. He was constantly following his wife around after he had passed. This upset the man's wife, as she felt his presence continuously and did not know how to help him. A good medium will sense and feel this immediately, and through the power of prayer may be able to help the confused soul move on to the higher vibration of the spirit world. An earthbound soul can also be helped, not only through the medium's prayer, but all prayers.

When our love link with a spirit is strong they may visit us from time to time. Although we may not physically see them, we can sense their presence. For example, they may move an object or flicker a light in a room, or waft a particular smell past our nose to gain our attention. This is especially true for loved ones whom we hold dearly in our hearts. You may not always see or hear them, but be reassured when you think of them, and say their name in your mind and pray for them, they will be ever present.

However, despite the fact that the spirit may be hovering near you in some of your activities, it is much easier for the spirit to come forward in the presence of a medium, simply because the medium is not emotionally involved and is often able to see, hear, and feel the spirit.

Q: When you convey messages to a client, exactly how do you hear them from the spirit world? Do you tell the client everything that you hear, exactly, word for word?

A: It is not my place to change the messages I hear. However, I believe it is my duty to convey messages to my client in a spiritual and positive manner. The guides work very hard to assure that the messages are delivered in a spiritually balanced manner. For example, if a person has strong health warnings, then it would be appropriate to suggest they visit their doctor for a thorough checkup. Clients ought to leave a medium feeling uplifted, knowing that they have received emotional healing, and even more importantly, knowing that the guidance and direction they have received has been delivered to them positively.

Q: Do people have free will to make their own life choices?

A: Yes, they certainly do, and when visiting a medium people often come to seek acknowledgment and confirmation of their plans. The spirit world will give guidance and direction, yet will never interfere or make a decision on behalf of the client. We must all make our own choices, and often our spiritual growth periods bring us rapid evolvement through our mistakes and disappointments in life. After all, we are human, and we are also where we choose to be in life.

Q: Do you find that a message of impact or a special person often pops in from the spirit world in the last minutes of a reading?

A: Yes, very often in the last few moments of a reading a vital connection is made by a loved one in the spirit world. Also, a vital piece of information may be given to the client in the last few seconds of the reading. It may well be that this piece of information is what the client has been waiting to hear.

Q: I have heard that there are seven levels of consciousness in the spirit world. When we pass over, to which level do we go?

A: On earth, we create our own heaven and hell, and it is essentially no different in the spirit world. We will evolve to the level of consciousness that we created while living on earth. For example, our good deeds of today hold us in good stead for tomorrow and beyond. I believe we live several lifetimes, and in each lifetime we lead by example. To progress spiritually we must learn to be kind, loving, compassionate, forgiving, understanding, and sympathetic, to name a few of the qualities we all must aspire to. By walking a strong pathway of light, many people could evolve to the fourth plane, which is labeled "the happy plane." They say that Jesus Christ evolved to the seventh plane.

Should a person choose a path of self-destruction by choosing crime and corruption on earth, then when the soul passes over they will reside in the lower planes. The lower planes are the planes between the earth plane and the spirit world. Eventually, these souls will see the light and be helped over to the first plane of consciousness in the spirit world.

Q: When a person commits suicide, where do they end up?

A: Through the love and prayers of family and friends after their passing, they will be helped through the veil. Sometimes after such a tragic passing, the spirit hovers around their physical body for a period of time, feeling lost and confused. They are generally helped to the spirit world by a loved one who has already passed over, who comes and takes them by the hand, guiding them to their plane of consciousness.

Sometimes a person who has lost a partner or child contemplates suicide themselves, as they cannot bear to be without their loved one. However, when taking their own life, they may not necessarily end up being with their loved one in the spiritual planes.

When altering one's destiny, we alter our karmic lessons and tests on earth that have been predetermined for us in each lifetime. Therefore, those committing suicide will then reincarnate back to earth and virtually restart the same process or life pathway that they had prior to their death.

Q: Should a person who commits suicide be cremated?

A: Not necessarily, unless this was a written or verbal request prior to the passing. If there are no instructions, then the family must decide.

Q: When you communicate with a person who has committed suicide, how are they?

A: There is confusion around them at first, as they try to show and tell me how they passed; however, some may not want to discuss their passing. Many souls who pass over in such tragic circumstances only wish to remember the happy times of their lives and desire to erase painful memories that they once experienced on earth. In some instances, it can be difficult for the spirit to make a clear communication as so much sadness is attached to their passing.

Q: Does a spirit always recall their last earthly experience?

A: Some only wish to remember or recall the happy times that they experienced during their previous lifetime. Others will recall and report all the details to me of their death, showing me strong colored pictures in my mind. Some will also report the last words they said before passing, or the last people they thought of before leaving.

Q: Tell me more about what it's like when a person comes to see you for a reading.

A: People come to see me for a variety of reasons. First, they have been recommended to me by word of mouth, as I never advertise. Often the person wishes to make contact with a loved one in the spirit world, and I feel so humble to be able to facilitate this for them. To me, the true work of a medium is to become the telephone connection between those on earth and those who have passed over into the spirit world, bringing forth messages of comfort, reassurance, and love from the other side. Having a reading with a good medium ought to result in an uplifting experience of sharing in love and light energy, and walking away with a new sense of well-being and peace. I cannot begin to describe to you the feeling of being able to talk to a child or teenager in the spirit world, and relay their personal messages to family. I thank God daily for this blessing. When a mother is weeping on her knees for her son to return to earth, I feel so humble to try and ease some of her pain by relaying messages of love and truth from the spirit world.

Q: When a person passes over, how long is it before they are able to make contact through a medium?

A: It can vary from minutes to days, weeks, months, or even years. It can also depend on how spiritually aware the person was before they passed over. I have had spirits contact me only hours after their passing. Some spirits have communicated with me, telling me that their physical body is still in the mortuary awaiting their funeral service; they will describe their time and place of death, giving full graphic details of their passing.

Q: When talking with a spirit, for what length of time can they stay chatting with you?

A: Sometimes it is a few moments, other times a spirit can chat for an hour. It also depends on the communication skills of the spirit and how the medium's energy is at the time of communication. In other words, if the medium is getting tired, then the contact with the spirit can start to fade, and hearing the spirit may start to become more static. The spirit will remain chatting for only as long as they desire to. If the love link is strong between the spirit and my client, then we could have a good one-hour session together. It is all orchestrated very naturally; a spirit just pops in when they feel the medium is ready.

Q: Do you actually feel or see the death of a person? For instance, if a person has been shot, do you physically feel it, as well as see it?

A: Yes, I am often shown a vision of how the person died. I can also feel their physical pain prior to their passing. If they have been shot, then I will feel the pain where the bullet or bullets have entered their body. If a person passes with lung cancer, while I am talking with them I will usually run out of breath and know that they had lung problems. Regularly, I ask the spirit to step back and release the physical feelings of pain that I feel on their behalf.

Q: When an elderly lady has suffered from Alzheimer's prior to her passing, does she communicate from the spirit world showing her disease?

A: At first she will make contact showing me her confusion, and how she felt while living with Alzheimer's. Often these messages are relayed with a great sense of humor; for instance, she will say she is lost and will give me strong indication that she was not coherent prior to her passing, but that she was, however, happy prior to her passing, and this will come through strongly. Once she has identified her presence to her loved one, then she will start a clearer communication. She must show me her medical condition prior to her passing, even though she has now been fully healed, and her spirit will then revert back to show me a younger age where she would have experienced good health on earth.

Q: When a person dies, where do they go in spirit?

A: Before evolving to the plane of their consciousness, the spirit often goes to a healing bay in the spirit world. This is a place where they gather comfort and information from the guardian angels and healers in the spiritual realms. For example, some people pass over instantly and can become disoriented. Children may feel lost after a sudden death. However, we are always met and helped over. The angels in the healing bays will nurture the soul emotionally, helping them to understand where they are, and the spiritual process, before the soul moves on to their designated plane.

Q: Can you communicate with animals that have passed over?

A: Yes. It is exciting when animals make a strong communication. I have had conversations with horses, parrots, goats, dogs, and cats. During a reading I am often shown a pet sitting beside their loved ones. Even though they now reside in the animal kingdom in the spirit world, our pets will still accompany us or visit us in life, remembering and maintaining the love link once shared on earth.

Q: When a spirit is anxious to come through for the first time, does their emotional condition block the communication?

A: No, not really. Sometimes I have to work harder to raise my level of consciousness to make a clearer connection. On occasion the spirit may have followed a certain religion that did not believe in the life-hereafter; when this type of situation occurs the communication between the spirit and the medium can be a little strained.

When the spirit has stepped in close to me, I feel chills run throughout my physical body. The strong emotional feelings of my client can sometimes block a communication. It is as though the person has a cloud of grief sitting above their head, and this can often be cleared away during a session. Also the spirit has to be ready to make a connection, which often comes with messages of love, joy, and peace for my client.

Q: Do those who communicate from the spirit world come through on a faster vibration?

A: Yes, the spirit world operates on a much faster vibrational wave length. And it is my spirit guide who works very hard to balance the level of vibration between the spirit and myself. This enables me on most occasions to hear voices clearly. I can hear them speaking to me in normal tones, as though we were old friends having a chat or cup of tea together.

Q: When a person crosses over into the spirit world, do they wait for other family members to be reunited before they reincarnate?

A: It is my understanding that when we have a strong love link with a family member, they will often wait to regroup with their love links in the spirit before they re-incarnate. Please take into consideration that timing has no meaning in God's world. Fifty years on earth is like a flash of an eyelid for spirit. If the love link is strong between family members, then I believe that those in the spirit world will wait and prepare for our homecoming when the time is right.

11

Letters of Love

I am loved.
I am safe.
A part of my self watches over me.
I know.
I am.
The light is with me.
God is real. God is.
Nothing is wrong.
I am at peace.
Things are OK.
I can love.
Everything is one.

The Path to Love
—Deepak Chopra

I feel so blessed to receive many wonderful letters of thanks, love, and encouragement from my clients. I have selected the following letters to share.

Dear Jenny,
I found my first experience of a spiritual reading absolutely "mind blowing."

To discover that there were lost loved ones still walking with me in this life was incredibly moving and inspiring.

At a time when I seemed to be struggling on all fronts, being reassured of positive future outcomes lifted a huge weight and enables me to focus so much more clearly on my true path.

As a counselor, I might say that such a reading is rewriting one's life script, and provided it is positive I can see only good in such an experience.

"Balance" is something I consider to be important, not only in my clients' lives, but also my own.

For me, having a reading has helped me to keep my spiritual, emotional, and physical lives in balance, a sort of three-way counseling session.

It is an experience that has left me feeling reassured and excited about what I can achieve.

I believe a spiritual reading given by a reputable practitioner is one of many pathways one can use on the journey of self-discovery.

I shall always be grateful to you, Jenny, for allowing me to share in your gift.

May God always be with you,

Alison

Dear Jenny,

Approximately seven years ago, my husband had a reading with you, and much to his delight his meeting with a fair-haired lady with two boys came true. And much to my delight, it was me. You told him it would be a long and meaningful relationship, leading to marriage, and that we would live in a two-story house with views of the water. He had no children at the time and his personal life was in disarray when he came to see you. Being in his early thirties, he was lonely and desperate to settle down with a family. You told him he would have two children of his own, a son and daughter, and two stepsons.

About a year after meeting my husband I came to see you. A lot has obviously happened since our last meeting, but the outcome has been just exactly as you told us. We have a lovely two-story home with magical views of the water in the exact location you told me. Along with my two sons we now have had a beautiful daughter and will keep you posted on the arrival of another son.

Plus, other details you told us both have come true. You told me about two uncles of mine in the spirit world who walk with me in life; I did not even know them and my mom has since confirmed and told me about my two uncles.

I am so grateful to you for fitting me in to your busy schedule. Thank you.

God Bless

Karyl

Dear Jenny,

In 1991 I came to see you for a reading. I went home from the reading feeling wonderful. This is something you did for me when you read for me. You gave me a wonderful lift when I felt a little down.

I was always wanting to share my reading with family, in particular my mother-in-law (Dawn). Well, in this particular reading you mentioned Dawn's sister, June, who passed over ten years ago. We were very special people to June. She always called my husband her favorite nephew. June came into the reading you gave me and sent her love to Rosemary. I did not know who Rosemary was but when I shared the reading with Dawn, she knew who Rosemary was. Dawn said to me, "Stop the tape. Now rewind it and let me listen to that part again."

"Well," she said, "how did she know about that? No one but June and I knew about Rosemary. It has been a secret we have kept for some fifty years."

Dawn went on to tell me her sister June had given birth to a baby girl and adopted her out at birth and called her Rosemary and never told anyone else in the family. She then asked me to keep it a secret also, which I did.

Dawn passed over in 1993. In 1995, I went to my letter box, and there was a letter from the Timaru Young Person's Court. I knew the letter was for Dawn and not for me. The post office must have thought it was mine, as not

only did we have the same first and last names
but we also lived next door to each other. We
both used a different first name, but if we received mail by our correct first names it was
easy for the post office to mix our mail up. As
Dawn had passed over I was not sure what to
do at first; then I thought, well, I don't want
to upset my father-in-law, so I had best open
the letter and deal with it myself.

Rosemary had hired someone to trace her
family. I had to read the letter twice to believe
it. I then recalled Jenny's reading from 1991
and thought, this is wonderful. I then rang
Timaru to speak with Rosemary and told her
she had the right contacts and that unfortunately all of Rosemary's family had passed
on except one uncle in New Zealand and one
full brother living in Texas. I told her I would
contact them both, and if they wished to meet,
I would arrange the contact. I contacted the
brother in Texas; he was absolutely delighted,
and they have talked on the phone and
swapped photos but are yet to meet in person.
Their birth certificates confirmed they were
full brother and sister. Rosemary's only regret
is that she did not try to find her family
sooner.

This only goes to prove that there is life
after the physical body dies.

Jenny, you are a caring, lovely, beautiful
lady, and I feel it is a real privilege to have
met you and have you read for me. The joy I
received from bringing two people together is

something that I cannot put into words, but
through meeting you, not only did you light
up my life but I was able to light up someone
else's life also. And that is what life is all about,
sharing.

Love,

        Pauline

I received this wonderful note in a card from a client
named Lesly.

Her card said:

We are united in a timeless circle of love
My love is with you.

At the time I saw Lesly she was approximately thirty
years of age and had been born with spina bifida. She
has not been held back by any physical restrictions and
is an extremely gifted, loving, and intelligent young
lady. Meeting Lesly and sharing in her bright light
touched my life. She is truly one of the dearest and
most precious souls I have ever met. Because of her
physical disabilities her spiritual awareness has been
heightened in such a way that I feel she teaches and
helps young and old onto their spiritual pathways.
When I met Lesly, unbeknownst to me she had lost her
best and most loving friend, her Mother! Her card went
on to say:

Dear Jenny,

First and foremost I would like to thank you from the bottom of my heart for enabling me to speak with my mom. As I'm sure you know, we were as close as a mother and daughter could be, and you helped illuminate the dark and tortuous tunnel of losing a loved one. For that I am forever grateful.

All my love,
　　　　Lesly,
　　　　Pasadena, USA

Dear Jenny,

I found reading your book, *Through the Eyes of Spirit*, amazing. Here was someone who believed the same as me. It made me cry a happy cry. I just couldn't put it down. You are right, we all need to share the light and love that is given to us.

This world of ours is full of so much evil and pain. It's so nice to connect with your warmth and energy. You have a gift that words cannot explain, and something that I would like to be able to give out myself one day. Your gift shines through in your book, and for this I sincerely thank you.

Take care and God Bless,
　　　　Marge
　　　　Waitara, New Zealand

Dear Jenny,

Just a thank you, and I wish to share some affirmations of the "Reading" you gave to me on the 12th of March, 1991. You told me that my father's seventieth birthday would turn into a family reunion and it did. You also mentioned that I would have to be careful with my physical body because of sciatica pain. Since I have seen you I have had two spinal fusions.

The family names you mentioned, Judith, Katherine, and Elizabeth (Betty) were all relevant to my family.

You mentioned my adopted daughter who is now twenty-three years of age. You told me that she would meet up with my son and they would get on well. They met up a few weeks ago and related to each other beautifully. So thank you, Jenny, for a very positive and uplifting reading.

Yours sincerely,

Sandy

I always find my work exciting, especially when I receive feedback from people who have gotten interesting messages from the spirit world. At the time of their reading, they may not fully understand the message given, and clarity is often brought about by discussing their message with a close family member or friend. This was portrayed vividly in the following note I received from a beautiful lady named Helen.

Recently I attended a spiritual reading with
Jenny. In talking with Jenny about a week later,
on another matter, I shared a subsequent story
with her that had come from my reading.

During the course of my reading, an old
friend came through to chat. Her name is
Gwen and she passed over about twelve
months ago. Gwen was coming forward, saying that it was the first time she had contacted
anyone after passing away. But she was happy
and contented over there, and had at last found
Peter, and they were walking together in the
green valleys and high mountains as free spirits. This message made me feel very happy,
although at the time, I was unsure who Peter
was. But it was good to think that she was not
alone, happy, and still had her delightful sense
of humor.

About three or four days after my reading
with Jenny, I decided to contact a mutual
friend of Gwen's and mine in Matamata, to
see if she could shed light on who Peter was.
She laughed when I relayed the message in
my reading about Gwen. She said that she had
been dreaming of Gwen for the past three
nights, walking in the green fields and mountains, being free, happy, and with her friend
Peter. For you see, Gwen had never married,
and had apparently met Peter when she was a
young woman. Peter desired very much to
marry Gwen, however she had a valid and private reason for not doing so. Peter understood
this, and found that her reason did not matter

to him. He was so in love with her and wanted desperately to get married. Alas, Gwen never changed her decision, and went through life living alone.

Sadly, Gwen and Peter never married, and it was to Helen's delight when she found out the true message given in her reading. It was a happy ending, or maybe beginning, for Gwen and Peter are now together in the spiritual realms of peace and love. This simple message, relayed from Gwen in the spirit world, was a way of letting her friends know she was once again reunited with Peter, the only man she truly loved.

Dear Jenny,

I am still amazed and eternally grateful for the healing you gave me.

I asked my husband a couple of weeks ago if he thought I had changed at all since my reading. He replied, "You seem more at peace."

I am still astounded at the healing you gave me. I received clarity. I had been mulling over these deep, dark thoughts. Now colors even appear brighter! I feel that you healed me of a very deep depression. I knew I had been deeply saddened by my mother's death (she was and is still my best friend), but I had no idea of the extent of my depression. I used to cry several times a week and now I can truthfully say, even though I still miss her and think of her daily, I can smile inside because I know she is all right, and she is with me. Jenny, you remarked to me that I would probably go home and cry. I did not. As a matter of fact, I felt euphoric!! Actually it was at that time the pine trees seemed greener and the skies bluer!

I had never had a reading, and while I believed that there are gifted people such as yourself in the world, I never dreamt of meeting such a person, and having my lifelong questions answered. In fact, I was referred to you by Robin who at that time was just an acquaintance. One day while I was playing in the park with my children she approached me and told me about her reading with you. She had told no one else about her reading but said she felt she needed to share it with me. I since believe that an angel brought her to me! And to me, Robin is an example of an angel here on earth!

When I was a small child, I remember vividly conversations with my mother regarding life after death. I was raised in a strict but loving Catholic home and attended parochial schools, both in elementary and high school. While my mother tried to reassure me that there was life after death and, of course, I would see her again, the deep, dark question remained. What really happened after you died? I did not believe in life after death until meeting you. Unfortunately, I am an individual who had to have it proven to them, and by all means you did. There is no longer any doubt in my mind about life after death. I now know there is. That is why I am eternally grateful to you and ever so thankful for the gift of healing that you gave me. I am a new person because of meeting you and I look forward to seeing you again this year.

You remarked that my mother was proud of me, and that she was calling for "Clara" and that is my aunt who is soon to pass.

You told me that we had two homes for sale (which we did), and that one would sell shortly (which it did). You also stated that we would move into a large, white, and bright home. We are closing the end of the month on our new large, white, and bright home!

And you told me many more precious items in my reading!

Thank you again from the bottom of my heart!

Love,

Mary Scarcello

Dear Jenny,

I came to your home on Sunday, February 11th, after having seen Colin Lambert for a healing session. My husband, Bruce, and I were visiting New Zealand from upstate New York, and I was determined after reading your book, *Through the Eyes of Spirit,* to have a reading with you.

I just wanted to let you know how very much I appreciate the time you took from your Sunday to give me a reading. I have listened to my tape several times and it is

amazing how accurate you were with so many
things. You described my daughter and baby
granddaughter so accurately. You connected
with my sister, who was twenty years older
than I and died from breast cancer. You said
that we resembled each other and said that her
hair appeared white to you, although she may
have lost it before she passed on. That was
exactly correct, as was your diagnosis of cancer.
You connected with my mother, who passed
on from kidney failure after many years of
suffering from Alzheimer's. You said that she
had trouble communicating before she passed
on and did not realize where she was going
when she passed over, and that too was exactly
as it was. You connected with my brother and
said that he had passed on very quickly and
was initially confused about what had happened and where he was.

My brother did, indeed, pass on very
quickly. He was killed in a car accident.

You connected with my father, who had
died of a heart attack when he was only forty-
eight years old, and said that he had gotten
things done quickly in his life, as though he
knew he didn't have much time, and that he
had stayed near his family like a guardian
angel. You then mentioned a family member
who had been in a serious auto accident and
touched your forehead, mentioning a scar. My
niece, who is one year younger than I am, had
been in an auto accident and had a scar from
it in exactly the spot you were touching. She

had told me that after coming out of her coma, she had seen my father's spirit each night by her bedside and that he had told her repeatedly that she would recover and that the baby that she was expecting at that time would also be fine (something her doctors had considerable doubt about). Everything my father told her came to pass.

Speaking of things coming to pass, several things you stated in the reading have already occurred. You said that our son would be calling us soon with good news and that he would be accepted for his Masters degree program; that is just what happened.

I could go on and on, because there was more in the reading, but I am sure you can see why I was so very pleased with your reading. When your second book comes out, please let me know how I can purchase it.

Please let me know if you ever come to New York. Thank you so much, Jenny. You have a wonderful gift and I was very privileged to experience it. I hope to hear from you again.

Sincerely,

Karen

I don't always remember what happens in a reading, so it is soul food for me to hear back from a client when a reading has hit the mark, because it reaffirms I am working in the spirit of love.

12

Meditation

Meditation is the art of listening. When you
pray, you are talking to God. When you meditate, you are listening to God.

Change We Must
—Nana Veary

*M*y work requires a great deal of energy
and I have found meditation to be the key
to a positive pathway of love and guidance from the
higher realms.

Meditation has helped me to fine-tune my connection with the spirit world, enabling me to work
on raising my vibrational level. It has helped me to
receive and pass on to my clients vital healing and
understanding from the spirit guides who work
with me.

The benefits of meditation have been insurmountable to me, and I highly recommend you take time
out of your busy schedule to enjoy the benefits and
reap the rewards of raising your personal level of
spiritual awareness by meditating regularly.

Meditation is self-realization in God. God is love, and God is within each and every one of us. Learning to meditate will teach you how to concentrate and focus your attention toward the God within, away from distractions. You need not be a religious person to do so, for the God within can be accessed at any given time. You do not have to go to church to gain this self-realization; rather, through regular meditation you will begin to harmonize with yourself. The harmony and vibration you create for yourself through meditating will mean you have created your own church within your heart, for this is where the real place of worship begins. Our actions speak louder and spread farther than words.

By meditating regularly you will pass on a bright inner light to all those with whom you come into contact. You will feel an overwhelming inner peace entering your life and filling your heart with feelings of wisdom, happiness, love, truth, and light. By stilling the mind and feeling calm and relaxed, you are allowing the light and love to enter your entire being. This light and love will fill every cell of your mind and body. We have the ability to manifest negative or positive thoughts. Through regular meditation you will be guided by God in a positive manner and allow your own free will to make clearer choices in life.

I believe that we each came back to the earth plane to gain God-consciousness. Through trusting in the higher power and letting go of our worries and cares,

we will gain so much strength and spiritual understanding. When we meditate we do this. In our silent
times we let go of all our worries and cares. Having an
inner recognition and awareness that each and every
one of us is a collective part of this Divine connection
will surely change and brighten up our world.

Through meditation we can recognize the Christ
within ourselves and, in turn, start to look at others in
a different light. In doing so, this recognition can give
an abundance of healing within ourselves and to all
those with whom we come into contact. By meditating,
we are recharging our batteries and brightening our
own inner light.

Through the art of meditation we can begin to send
our ideas and thoughts out to the spirit world, and in
doing so they will be met with a positive response. We
may require healing of our mind, body, and soul, and
we can receive this by meditating.

We each take so much for granted in this life; we
must all learn to pray and give thanks in our day-to-day
lives, and we can do this daily in our time of meditation. To learn the art of meditation one must first experience a stillness of the mind and body.

Open up your heart and soul to God's kingdom of
love and healing, and as you begin to meditate, feel an
enormous surge of love entering your entire being. We
must listen to God as we meditate and receive the messages that will enable us to develop our spirituality and
creativity. As we still our minds and sit or lie quietly, we

enter a new realm of consciousness, a realm that will unfold many answers and truths to each person who takes the journey of meditation.

We are all part of the Divine plan, and as we learn to tune in more to our conscious awareness, each person will feel the God within starting to manifest a new beginning in life. As you begin to meditate on a regular basis, achievements will be made in many areas of your life. Meditation will fill you with a renewed source, and you will experience feelings of peace and unconditional love. These feelings will engulf you for days and even months after some of your meditations. Always remember that our mind is the most powerful tool, so it is good to think kind and caring thoughts about others and send them love in your meditations. This love and light will be transmitted back to you, like a beacon connected to your soul. Our thoughts project as mirror images for ourselves; this is why it is good to learn forgiveness and unconditional love.

Through regular meditation we can learn to go within more and start to become in tune with our higher selves. Our higher selves do not carry an ego, but instead help us to walk a spiritual pathway of simplicity. As we become more in tune with our higher selves through the art of meditation, we will then appreciate and learn that perhaps our soul-purpose in this lifetime is to help others, setting aside our own grievances and moving forward in life on a selfless pathway.

By meditating you are creating harmony and balance in your lives. You will gain more spiritual awareness as your spirit teachers gather around you and communicate in your meditation. Not only do we receive communication from the spirit world; it will also enable us to become better communicators.

As you continue to meditate, know that your pathway will always be in the light; you will be guided and protected. Say a prayer in each of your meditations, asking for the God Power to surround Mother Earth and give her healing and upliftment. Not only are you meditating for yourself but also for the Universe, and your meditations will contribute toward planetary healing.

There are different methods and many forms of meditation—personally I find that simplicity is the key. I may sometimes sit or lie on the floor or a couch and drift off to music or just take some silent time. I always begin meditation with an opening prayer first, as I wish to seek guidance, love, and light from the higher realms. Some people prefer to sit upright in a chair with their feet firmly on the floor and their hands placed on their laps with palms facing upward. It is wise to concentrate your attention on the point between the eyebrows in the middle of your forehead. This is the third-eye area or Christ center, and as you concentrate your thoughts and attention toward this area, you will start to feel a calmness around you. You have started to tune in to your spiritual eye. Do not rush your meditation time, but rather sit for a few moments quietly and begin to tune into the stillness that is manifesting in your surroundings. A strong method of learning to concentrate while meditating is to listen to your breath. As you do so, focus your thoughts and attention on the sound of your breathing; this will relax you very quickly.

Meditation is sacred to each and every one of us, and the more you still your mind, the more you will develop. Twenty minutes a day would be wonderful for each individual; some people who are dedicated meditate at sunrise and sunset. Do it at whatever time is best for you, but remember also that we live in a world of reality and cannot stay in this wonderful meditative state all day. Certainly we will be filled with an inner peace and feel the benefits of our meditation; however, it is most important to become grounded again after meditating. Those who are in a half-in and half-out meditative state can sometimes find it hard to get on with the practical side of life. After all, we came back to live and learn in this lifetime and must make sure that we are completely grounded in our day-to-day lives.

I have written some guided meditations, and I invite you to join me in reading them. Stay in these meditations for as long as you like, but remember, after meditating it is good to drink a glass of water; this will help to cleanse and ground you. Also make sure you are well-grounded before you drive the car or get on with your day-to-day business. Some people may have to walk on the grass barefooted for a moment or two to become fully grounded and completely back in their physical bodies.

Enjoy your meditation as it is a precious time for you to invest in yourself—a time to gain understanding and receive healing from the higher realms. As you meditate, reap the benefits of allowing the God Love to fill every cell of your entire being.

Dolphin Island Meditation

I want you to find a comfortable chair, a couch, a bed, or lie on the floor. Find your most comfortable position before you begin this meditation.

Feeling relaxed, I want you to concentrate on the words being spoken to you. Listen carefully and harmonize with the music you are playing. Take in a few deep breaths, in through your nose with positive energy, and breathe out through your mouth any negativity that you may have been experiencing. Listen to your breath, focusing on each one.

I am going to take you on a short journey. Before we begin, clear your mind of any unwanted thoughts. Lock them behind a large, secure door and bolt it, or throw them over a waterfall. This meditation will give you upliftment and a great surge of energy.

Just feel yourself relaxing and floating; you are well-protected and cared for, surrounded by love and light energy. Ask to be protected by the Christ Light, and know that this meditation will bring forth a wonderful new energy surge that will enter your whole being. Again, take in a few more deep breaths, and concentrate on your breath. I want you to focus on the area between your eyebrows; this is your third-eye area. With your eyes closed, visualize that you can see this eye in the middle of your forehead.

Imagine that your third eye has been sleeping and closed for some time, and now it is starting to open. Your third eye is the seat of your psychic eye, and as you begin to open up this area, you will be able to visualize more of your life pathway.

Feeling relaxed, we are going to take a journey across water. The day is perfect, clear, warm, and calm. A nice sea breeze is blowing in gently. Let us walk toward the jetty, where a very large, luxurious, safe, and comfortable boat awaits.

As you board the boat, you feel happy and relaxed about your journey beyond. When you are aboard, you have your own seat, with a spare seat beside you. This seat has been reserved for whomever you would like to take along with you on this spiritual and uplifting journey; just say their name in your mind and visualize them receiving the same uplifting energy given to you.

You feel such excitement and bliss as you sit on the boat, which sweeps calmly through the crystal clear water. The sun is gleaming and sparkling on the water, like tiny crystals or diamonds, just sparkling on this deep blue sea.

Come over to the rails and look down into the water. You see that a family of dolphins is swimming on either side of the boat; they are singing and whistling to one another. Just looking at them, you feel their joy and happiness. You know that you are being guided by the dolphins toward a safe sanctuary. Stay by the rails and enjoy watching the dolphins for a few moments as you are guided along.

As we venture along further, we come into a calm and beautiful bay. The dolphins have followed us in here. The captain asks if you would like to take a swim with the dolphins on this warm day.

As you enter the water and start to swim with the dolphins, it is as though you have an understanding of the communication they give to one another. They seem to sense your thought patterns as you swim with them, play with them, and talk with them, and you feel your energy level soaring even higher. You can feel the healing surging into every cell of your entire being.

As you swim, you dip your head in and out of the water, feeling safe and protected. It is just you and the dolphins swimming around in perfect harmony. Immerse your head in the saltwater now, to give your aura a good cleansing. Stay in the warm water for a few minutes. Swim a little more, and when you are ready, board the launch again. As you dry off in the warm sunshine, bid the dolphins a fond farewell. They will understand, and remember, you can come swimming with them at any time you desire, just by connecting with this meditation.

As we near the second jetty, you notice the shoreline has an extra sparkle to it, as though you can feel this wonderful positive energy flowing forth and touching you while still on the launch.

As you step ashore into this sanctuary, you are awed by the colorful bird life and exotic trees and flowers. Everything is so green and lush. As you look around, you can feel the quiet, the peace and tranquility that engulfs you by just being here. Stay here for five minutes or so and soak up this healing calm.

Walking along a little further, you see a large waterfall, cascading over the cliffs beyond. Underneath this waterfall is a lovely clear pond, surrounded by beautiful rock formations and ferns overhanging the edge of the pond. The water is so clear and clean, you can see to the bottom. The water temperature is lukewarm and very comfortable, so you can swim and wash away the saltwater that you still have on you. The clearness of the water indicates how your life will become crystal clear to you, as you feel the upliftment entering your mind and body.

You will find that a great cleansing is taking place as you swim and laze in this pond, lingering for a while to rejuvenate your soul.

This place is near perfection; the colors of the flowers surrounding the pond are identical to the colors of the rainbow. You climb out of the water now and lie on the warm rocks, feeling the healing power of the sun's magnificent energy touching every cell of your body and soul, charging them with powerful positive energy. Stay here for five minutes.

It is time to leave this pond, and you feel a little sad as you walk through the beautiful sanctuary on your way back to the boat. It is hard to leave this invigorating, healing place. However, you are also joyous, knowing that you carry that energy deep within your own soul. You can ride on this launch at any time, swim with the dolphins, bathe in the waterfall pond, and accept spiritual blessings as often as you choose.

It is now time to make your way back slowly from this meditation, as you reboard the launch and come back across the water. You arrive at the jetty with a new sense of well-being and much higher energy: the upliftment is indescribable joy.

On the count of five, I want you to start coming back slowly; on the count of four, slowly, slowly becoming a little more aware. On the count of three, become aware of your surroundings; on the count of two, move your hands, eyes, and feet, slowly, slowly; on the count of one, open your eyes, becoming aware of your surroundings.

Sit or lie quietly for a while, reflecting on all the energy you have received.

Native American Village Meditation

Come and join me on this inspirational meditation that will take you on a journey to help you receive healing and upliftment.

Please find a comfortable position in which to meditate as we take this journey together. Please concentrate and shut out any outside noises as we enter this meditation together.

As you take this time out for yourself, feeling relaxed and completely at ease, just feel yourself drift off into a peaceful state of well-being. If you have some background Native American music to play it would be ideal for this meditation.

Feeling relaxed, concentrate on the words as you are guided through this meditation.

Take some gentle breaths in and out, feeling comfortable, feeling yourself unwind, and letting go of any outside noises or interference. Relax and keep breathing, in and out, in and out.

Imagine that we have stepped straight into a Native American village, just as the villages used to be, way back in time. As you step into this village, we want you to know that you are completely protected and surrounded by the white light. Feel this light engulf you, and visualize this white light streaming in from the top of your head to the tips of your toes. You are completely protected by the light of Christ.

As you step into the village, you see a chief walking toward you. He is coming to welcome you. It is as though you recognize him from the past.

Look around as he walks toward you; see the magnificently painted tipis, hear the children's laughter, and watch them at play. See the young warriors sharpening their arrowheads and talking among themselves. See the women chatting happily as they gather firewood and wash their clothes in the fresh stream that runs down from the mountains. Look around and see the men talking and planning the next buffalo hunt. Stay there, taking in your surroundings, for five minutes.

Now, as the chief approaches you, you find that he definitely looks familiar, and he is inviting you to come and sit with him and share the medicine pipe, along with the other men sitting around a large fire that has been built within a circle of smooth, round rocks.

Just being in this place, you can already feel a great surge of energy and healing. Look and see which tribe you are visiting. Do you recognize anyone else?

The chief is talking to you, telling you of the land, and how none of us really own the land, that the earth is for all of us to share. He talks to you of the Great Spirit, and the important role that spirituality has in our lives. Stay there, talking and listening for a few minutes.

He asks if you would like to take a canoe and paddle down the mountain stream that runs alongside the village. He picks out a beautiful canoe for you to use. You will see, as you paddle, that the water is clear and calm. The water imparts a strong feeling of cleansing to you as you take this short journey downstream. The beauty surrounding this stream is majestic, and the tall pine trees lining the stream are gently waving to you in the breeze.

As you look around the beautiful countryside, you are reminded by the chief of the Indian philosophy of wisdom from the Great Spirit. We should know that this spirit is within all things, the trees, the rocks, the grasses, the rivers, the mountains, the air we breath, the animalss and the flying birds.

You beach your canoe near a thick, grassy meadow. The Indians have left their horses grazing here; they are quite content to feed. Do you see the beautiful white horse standing with the other horses, looking so majestic? You are welcome to take a ride on this horse, back to the village, feeling comfortable and safe on its broad, strong back.

So much about this village seems so familiar to you; it is as though you have been here before.

The chief asks if you would like any special healing, or if you desire any holistic medicine while you are here visiting. He introduces you to the tribe's medicine man, a powerful healer. If you have an ache or pain, or something troubling you, ask for this holistic medicine, ask for this healing, and see what is being handed to you. Stay here for five minutes or so.

All around you is a great deal of activity. So much is happening all at once. Yet everyone is moving in a calm, focused, happy manner. You feel a part of this big happy family. You enjoy this feeling of community.

It is so good to be here, as you watch the sun set in the west. As dusk falls, the camp fire brightens and glows in the crispness of the evening air. Sit for awhile near the stream, and enjoy the peace and tranquility of this healing place.

The scent of cooking food draws you back to the fire. Listen to the chanting and the music; join in with the dancing around the fire! You can see yourself, leaning backward and forward, dancing, first one leg bent in the air, and then the other. This is truly an uplifting and joyous time for you, as you link with the people.

You understand perfectly the language being spoken, as you return to sit by the camp fire. Look and see who is sitting beside you; ask their name.

As you eat and talk, you experience a great surge of healing from the chanting and music. You wish you could stay here for a long, long time.

You sit and connect with the elders and feel respect flowing through you, as they teach and share with you their experiences of the past. So much wisdom and knowledge is being imparted to you. You feel a strong connection with nature and the naturalness of your surroundings. It is such an uplifting and comfortable feeling. Stay here a little longer.

The moon has risen very high, and the hour is growing late. It is time to thank your Indian friends for the time you have spent with them and to tell them all goodbye. As you prepare to depart, the chief hands you a gift, a present to take with you. You feel so happy, so filled with the joyous spirit of nature and community.

Wishing everyone a fond farewell, and coming back very slowly, on the count of five you say your goodbyes. On the count of four, you are feeling uplifted and ready to come back, slowly, slowly. On the count of three, feel yourself coming back, and on the count of two, feel your arms, legs, and feet move. On the count of one, your eyes gently open and you become aware of your surroundings. Take a little time to completely focus and sit relaxed, reflecting on the magical place you have just visited.

True Love Meditation

This meditation will take you onto the pathway of true love, joy, and happiness.

You will experience feelings of love from within that you may never have experienced before.

I want you to find a comfortable chair or a couch, and sit or lie in a position most relaxing and comfortable to you. Take your phone off the hook if you do not wish to be disturbed.

I want you to concentrate on the words being spoken to you, or if you are reading this meditation, to read it through slowly. You are well-protected, as the white light of God enfolds you, and the power and love of God protects you. Enjoy the feeling of being relaxed and free as we begin to move in the light together.

Take in some deep breaths; in through your nose and out through your mouth. Keep breathing in and out, deeply in and out. You feel yourself ready to drift off, leaving any worries you have behind you, and switching off any background or outside noises.

As you concentrate on this meditation, feel the love starting to well up inside you. Visualize this love flowing into you from a higher source. Allow the love to flow in through the top of your head. Imagine the top of your head is like a flower that has been sleeping or closed; open up this flower and allow the sunshine and love to reach you. This flower will stay open, and thus you will be receptive to the love energy flowing through you.

You may have some feelings stored deep within you, from past and present experiences, and now is the time to focus on this love energy around you. Imagine that the love energy you see is a brilliant white light; breathe it in, allow this light to come into your flower and fill your body, from your head to your toes. Let this light fill your heart, bringing in a greater awareness and understanding; feel the love energy enter your entire body. Feel your vibration lifting and your conscious awareness starting to elevate. You are now feeling relaxed and a sense of well-being emanates from you.

Any feelings of heartache you may have been experiencing are now leaving your body, and the love energy is giving you healing around your heart chakra, located in the middle of your chest area.

You are being given a golden goblet to drink from. It is filled with pure love. Sip away at this drink and allow every inch of your mind and body to feel the great benefits of the love that is being given to you.

This is not a physical love being offered to you; this is love from a much higher source: infinite love. I want you to repeat after me, in your mind, "I am a beautiful soul, and I love myself." And again, repeat, "I am a beautiful soul, and I love myself." Give thanks and feel privileged to receive this love. The more love you can give yourself, the more others, too, can return your love.

Now I want you to visualize that you are being taken into a big room, a room filled with love and light. In this room you will see an old woman sitting on a magnificent chair in the corner. She and the chair are just glowing. She has a mist of white light surrounding her. Ask her name. She asks you to come closer and invites you to sit beside her. Tell her where your heart is not filled with love, and she will help you. You sense her kindness and gentleness and overwhelming wisdom. Tell her you are looking for true love. She is saying, "My dear, to find true love with others you must first seek true love from within yourself." While you are sitting next to her, she will reach out to you and help you understand and experience true love, which seeps deep into your heart. She offers you great peace and healing as she places her hand upon your right shoulder. Stay, talking with the old woman for five minutes or so.

She continues to speak with you. Ask her a question about true love. She is able to answer, for she has lived a long life and has had many experiences. She is very happy to talk to men and women, for she is unbiased; she is pure love and carries this essence from a higher dimension.

She says to you, "It is all so very simple. You arrive on the earth plane with nothing. You have chosen your parents to learn from, and as you grow, you learn and teach one another about love. As you go through some of life's lessons and walk forward in life, you search for true love. Look deep within, my dears, for true love is actually within all of you. True love is the essence of all." The old woman is very evolved and comes from a much higher dimension. She whispers to you, "I am Love, I am Love, I am Love."

She advises you to tell yourself that you are love, for God and love are one, and each individual is part of this cosmic and collective love, a love that gives our planet energy and life force and spreads a radiant light over each person who recognizes this love.

Stay in this magnificent place for a few moments and feel the love. This is a love that you may never have experienced before. This is infinite love, and it fills every cell of your entire being. This love will stay with you for eternity, a love that will take away feelings of sadness and loneliness, and a love that you can draw upon from deep within at any time, feeling comfort, peace, and serenity that will fill your whole being.

True love is given to us in life when the time is right, so relax, let go, and just go with the flow. As you breathe in this love, send it out to all those who may need love at this time. Speak their names in your mind, so they also receive the love you are experiencing. Your love can be sent to those in the spirit world or those living on the earth plane.

Remember that you can take this journey of true love at any time you desire, for it only takes a few minutes of your time each day. Be kind to yourself and fill up with true love each day. As you begin to make your way back from this meditation, you will know you have experienced true love, as you will feel totally consumed by this love, uplifted and ready to share your newfound energy and vibration in a very positive manner. You have experienced and will continue to experience true love from deep within. Remember, to enjoy life, we must take true love into our hearts, and when we serve humanity and help others it is not just a duty, for with love and kindness in our hearts, it is a joyful pleasure.

Now visualize a bright golden light surrounding your heart area, and feel that this light is a magnificent source of love for you. Stay, concentrating on filling your heart chakra in your chest area with this love and light for a few moments longer.

Now I want you to focus on the flower on the top of your head. Gently close this flower, knowing that you can reopen it and connect with true love whenever you choose.

Starting to drift back from this meditation now, bringing back an inner feeling of true love, on the count of five, listen and become aware that it is time to come back. Slowly, slowly, on the count of four, become aware that you are slowly moving back, and on the count of three, feel your hands and toes move. On the count of two, feel your eyes flicker and become aware of your immediate surroundings, and on the count of one, you are back in the room, fully aware of your surroundings. Now just sit or lie quietly where you are for a few moments. Relax, and remember, you can take this journey to link with your own true love that flows from within, at any time you choose.

Meeting Your Guardian Angels Meditation

This meditation will allow you to feel completely relaxed and uplifted, creating a time to leave all your worries and problems behind you. I want you to shut off from any outside noises or interferences; if you desire, take your telephone off the hook and avoid any distractions. Just relax, sit, or lie in the most comfortable position, and enjoy the peace and tranquility as this meditation is read to you. You can meditate day or night, so it is not necessary to sit in a dark room or light candles or play background music. This is a precious time you are taking to get in touch with yourself and link with your higher guidance.

I want you to concentrate on your breath, listen to your breath, and with each breath imagine that you are breathing in the Divine white light. As you breathe in through your nose, allow the positive energy to fill your entire being. Breathe out through your mouth, and release any negative energy buildup you may have within. Concentrate on your breath two or three more times. By now you are feeling lighter and starting to let go.

I want you to imagine that you are a feather, just blowing in a gentle breeze. See yourself lifting higher and higher, feeling lighter and lighter. Now visualize the top of your head like a flower, a beautiful flower of your choice. The area around the top of your head is your crown chakra area, and we wish to open up this area.

First, ask for the light, love, and power of God to engulf and protect you. I now want you to visualize the flower at the top of your head starting to open up, and as you do so, you will see a bright white light connecting above your head and flowing into your flower. As this light radiates above you and enters your body, you can feel the wonderful sensations that this light is filling you with. Each cell of your entire body is being filtered with this bright white light; this is the light of Christ. Already you feel that peace and tranquility have entered your soul, and you are starting to feel such joy and upliftment from this spiritual experience.

If at any time you feel tears flowing forth, then allow them to come through, as this is also a healing time for you. Your tears are a healthy cleansing; your tears are vital, for we must have them in order to fertilize the soil and allow the seeds of life to grow within our soul. As you feel yourself completely relaxed and letting go, I want you to once again ask for God's protection around you; just ask to be surrounded in God's light.

Remember, you are in control and well-protected as I take you on your spiritual journey to meet up with your guardian angels. Relax, and now take in another deep breath, in through your nose, breathing in positive energy, and out through your mouth, releasing from deep within any anxiety or negative buildup you may have stored.

Enjoy every moment you link with the spirit world, and when the time is right, you will be brought back from this meditation. This time of meditation will raise your level of consciousness and awareness; it's a wonderful time to connect with your higher self. Feel the light flowing through from the top of your head to the tips of your toes. See and visualize the white light within and surrounding your entire being.

Join me as I now take you on a beautiful journey, a journey of self-discovery, harmony, and great upliftment for your soul. Imagine that we are walking together along a narrow pathway. It is a warm and calm day, and as we begin our journey together, you notice the pathway is starting to widen very quickly. As we continue on, you sense the openness and bright light guiding you on this pathway. You feel completely safe and totally relaxed throughout this meditation. In the days and weeks following this time of upliftment for your soul, you will start to reap the benefits.

As you walk forward, you notice in the distance a beautiful garden surrounded by golden oak trees. Everything is bright and warm around you, and the colors you see are indescribable. You feel tremendous inner peace, seeping so deeply within. You are filled with so much love and light, and these feelings fill every cell of your entire being. Stay in this garden for five minutes.

As you continue your journey on this beautiful and enriching day, the sky is shimmering and sparkling with blue lights that look just like crystals. The sun reflects rays of light that glow and shine above you. The day is clear and warm, and you can see for miles ahead. Visualize your life being like this; imagine that you can see your way ahead clearly in life.

Only a few steps in front of you there is another garden. As you enter this garden, you are feeling light and breezy and the soft, cushiony moss pathway feels comfortable and springy underfoot. You see a sign above an archway as you enter the garden; it reads "The Garden of Tranquility." This is the garden of spirit, and the plant and bird life you see in front of you is beyond magnificence. Each colored flower seems to reach out and speak to you, and a deep sense of inner freedom overwhelms you in this place of beauty and tranquility. You can communicate with the plant and bird life, just by your presence and telepathic thought patterns. This is a beautiful cottage garden, planted by spirit; the birds and insects fly around you in a welcoming and loving way, enjoying your presence. You can feel yourself laughing inside as the joy and happiness of this magical Garden of Eden enters your soul. You see a comfortable garden seat in front of you. Go ahead and sit on the seat, and enjoy this magical slice of heaven for a few minutes.

Walking slowly forward again, into the garden, you come to a gate. As you step forward and open the gate, your spiritual guide is there awaiting your arrival, or you may have a loved one from the spirit world greeting you at this gate. He or she will now take you by the hand as you journey on. Look to see who is waiting for you; ask for a name and see how they are dressed. Your guide or loved one is greeting you with some words of wisdom. Ask them about your spiritual pathway and progression in this area. You may want to ask them a question about your material pathway in life. Take some time to stop and talk and gather answers to your questions. Stay here for a few minutes.

Continuing on, you see a large rainbow ahead; the magnificent colors within the rainbow seem to engulf you and fill you with healing. Reach out to this rainbow, and as you do so, see the colors, as soft as cotton candy. Place your hand within the rainbow and gently take a piece of rainbow in the color you desire to have this day. Drape this color around you; this is your cloak of enlightenment, healing, and love. This rainbow is very special and has a stairwell attached to it. Your guide permits you to enter the stairwell and climb higher. You begin to climb the steps, twelve steps in all. The healing and upliftment you feel is magical; total happiness is within you, and it is indescribable. This is truly a heavenly feeling, and you know your life is being touched in a positive manner at this moment. You are so privileged to be taking this journey today, and the energy surrounding and engulfing you is magnificent. You feel so much light and love around you and sense your soul being renewed from deep within. Happiness and sunshine filters in through the top of your head and flows through to the tips of your toes. Stay here for a few moments.

As you near the top of the stairwell, you see a large mirror. I want you to walk up to the mirror, look at yourself, and tell yourself, "I am a beautiful soul and I love myself." And again, walk up to the mirror and tell yourself, "I am a beautiful soul and I love myself." As you look at yourself in the mirror, take note of how you are dressed. Continue to look in the mirror and notice that your own image begins to fade. As you look again, you are now seeing a different face looking back at you.

This new face is your guide's face, greeting you. See if you can identify this person; ask them for a name. What type of clothing are they wearing? If you cannot see their face, then maybe you will see their hands.

Your spiritual guide is now handing you a gift. Look at your gift, accept it, and give thanks. Stay here for a few moments.

As you move on slowly, know that you will bring your gift back with you later. Now moving along this rainbow staircase, you are being given flowers by your guardian angels; you can see the colors of the flowers blending with your aura. This magnificent place you are visiting is an expansion of time, and everything feels so soft and light. At the very top of the stairwell is a door. I want you to walk toward this door that you see in front of you. The door is glowing and has a golden handle attached to it. Please open the door, and as you do, you will see that you have entered a room filled with golden light. Make a wish in this room filled with golden light. Everything in your life feels so clear to you now. Stay in the room of light as long as you desire.

As you move from the room of light, you notice another door to the right. Please enter this room. You can see the word Wisdom written above the door of this room. Look around and you will see many shelves, all lined with books. This is a library sectioned into four categories. The first category is Family History, the second is Past Lives, the third, Spiritual Teachings, and the fourth is Health. I want you to choose which section you wish to pursue, and your guide will lead you to the book of your choice. Hold onto your book, look at the cover, and see if you can read the title clearly. You will bring your book back with you later. Stay in the library of wisdom and knowledge for a few minutes longer.

It is time to journey on, and we have all linked together again. We have now been invited into the room of purification and healing, so remove your shoes as you enter this room and sit in the beautiful velvet chair provided for your comfort. Your feet are being soaked in a solution of warm lavender water. You feel so peaceful and rested, and as you sit, you see there is a priest in the room, calling your name and moving toward you. He is dressed in a purple cloak and is wearing a large gold cross around his neck. His hair and long beard are snow white. He is the Priest of Wisdom, and he offers you healing and purification. As you look at the priest, he is offering you the cup of Truth and hands you a cup of clear, pure water. He suggests that as you drink this water, you ask for healing in any areas where it may be required. You can request healing for your body, mind, or soul, whichever desires healing the most.

As you sip on this holy water you are filled with the brightest light of the most divine healing rays. This light is filled with sunshine, and this healing will benefit you greatly at this moment and in the future. Ask and you shall receive. Continue to receive the healing and love energy, and stay here for a few moments.

By now you are feeling full of warmth, and an abundance of energy is flowing through you. All of your problems and worries are leaving you as you linger in the spiritual realms. This is such a wonderful spiritual energy and journey you are experiencing. The universe is sharing with you as your guide takes you back to your pathway. Ask your guide to please give you his or her name, if you have not discovered your guide's name before. Ask your guide to give you any information that may be of relevance to you at this time. Stay here for a few moments. Thank your guide for this blessed time together, and ask them to stay close with you today and always as you make your way back along the pathway.

You feel such a magnificent feeling of upliftment and happiness—a feeling of well-being that you may not have experienced for some period of time. Again, give thanks for the healing you have received, and make your way back along the pathway slowly to join us. You will be counted back on the count of five, so bid your guide or whomever is present with you from the spirit world a fond farewell for the moment. Come back now slowly, on the count of four, slowly, slowly. On the count of three, feel yourself connecting back into your body, feeling relaxed and comfortable. Slowly, slowly, on the count of two, feel your eyes, your head, neck, and shoulder areas once again awakening. Now feel your arms, legs, and feet, your whole body gently relaxed. On the count of one, your eyes open slowly, slowly, and become fully focused on your immediate surroundings. Stay in this meditative position for a few moments, or as long as you desire, and reflect on the meditation and what you have just experienced during this precious time of taking time out for yourself.

If meditating in a group, you may like to share your meditations by asking the following questions:

- How many of you felt the lovely day and conditions around you and experienced the beautiful garden of spirit?

- Did you see your spiritual guide? Was there someone to meet you over the stile?

- Did you hear your spiritual guide's name?

- Did you ask about your spiritual, personal, and material pathways, and did you get an answer?

- Did you see and experience the rainbow? What color did you choose from the rainbow?

- Did you climb the steps? Did you see yourself in the mirror, or your guide's face in the mirror?

- Did you make a wish? See the library and select your category? Have you brought back a book in your mind with you?

- Did you see the priest, and what did he hand you?

- Did you feel healing and upliftment from this meditation?

- Remember, you can take this journey at any time you desire, by simply reading this meditation or having it read to you.

Dealing with Grief Meditation

During this meditation you may feel pain, anger, sorrow, and tears because of your loss. As you focus and listen to the words being spoken to you, I want you to know that this meditation is specifically designed to help you deal with and heal matters of the heart. I want you to say to yourself each day as many times as you can, "I have a happy heart, I have a happy heart. My heart is filled with love." Place your left hand in the middle of your chest, this is your heart chakra area, now place your right hand on top of your left, and feel the warmth penetrating through into your heart chakra area. Now with your hands in place, say again in your mind, "My heart is happy, My heart is filled with love, I release my sorrow to the Universe." As you sit for a moment and feel a gentle and warm vibration healing your heart, know that when you release your hands from your chest area, any anxieties will be removed. Not only will this be beneficial for you emotionally; it will also be very uplifting for you physically.

You may always feel a deep yearning in your heart, after the loss of a loved one, they have now gone on to a higher spiritual plane. Some of you may feel as though you would like to join your loved one, as your purpose to forge ahead in life feels as though it is diminishing. Remember that you must try very hard to continue to live, laugh, and be happy, as this would be the wish of your loved one in the spirit world. It is not your time to leave this precious lifetime. Try to be strong and turn every day in to a positive one. Begin working toward an acceptance that your loved one has now graduated to a higher plane of consciousness and peace.

Know that as you try to link with your loved one, it may be difficult for them to connect with you, as there are still too many emotions to deal with. Shortly after a passing you will feel them around you a great deal; your loved one will come in close to give you reassurance and comfort that they are truly healed. Sometimes it can prove difficult for them to link with you, especially if you have not been able to come to terms with their passing. However, be reassured that they will always try to filter their love back to you through the grief cloud you have above your head.

It does help to have a photograph out of a loved one; put a fresh flower in a vase beside their photograph, and ask them to accept the flower. If the flower is accepted, it will dry on the stem. Roses are especially good to use for this purpose.

The pain you experience from the grief of losing a loved one is personal. These feelings of pain can be indescribable, and at times no one else can truly understand or relate to how you are feeling. People sometimes say you will get over your loss in time, and time is a healer. However, I believe you never fully get over the loss of a loved one, as a piece of your emotional heart departs with them. You can learn to live with the emotional pain, and try to put your life back together in the best manner you can. If you can discuss your heartache with family and friends, this will definitely bring forth a great source of healing to you. Even if they do not always understand, at least you have been able to unload some of your feelings. This will help to clear away emotional blockages and allow your contact with the spirit world to become clearer and closer.

When you do come to a better place of acceptance and understanding, you will often feel their presence begin again. Be patient, for they will make contact with you when they feel the timing is appropriate. It is important at this moment to feel the presence of your loved one, rather than to see them in your mind's eye physically. Speak to them in your mind, and tell them you love them. You will feel the presence and love being returned to you. When you feel goose bumps or a chill running down your spine, know that this is when your loved one is present in the room. The chill you feel is your loved one connecting to your magnetic field or aura. This means they are right beside you.

Always remember that after your loved ones pass into the spirit world, they are only in the next room. It is agonizing, knowing that we can not physically touch them any longer or have a verbal conversation with them. However, they do hear you talking to them in your mind, or when you speak out loud; either way, they hear you and understand your thought patterns. And with practice you will hear them communicating answers back to you.

It is of little consolation knowing that we cannot just walk up to them and give them a big hug. However, it helps to know that they are at peace, safe, and joyful as they are now connected to a higher vibration.

You may have already spoken to or linked with your loved one in the sleep state. As you travel in the alpha state and drift from your physical body, your loved one comes forth from the spirit world to link with you. They will come to you in your dreams, bringing you love and comfort. This connection is made in the astral plane. As you drift off to sleep and rise from your physical body, you link up with your loved one in the spirit world. Often when you awaken the next morning after dreaming of a loved one, you may feel fulfilled and a great sense of peace connected to you, as they have shown you they are happy and now at peace.

Some mornings you will wake up and feel as though losing your loved one was just a bad dream or nightmare, only to realize that they have indeed gone on without you. Even though you are not together in the physical, your loved ones are near you, and watching over you, and they now serve as your helpful Angels.

They now protect and guide you on your pathway of life. They will give you strength in times of need and help to lift your morale when your heart is heavy and sad.

Before you enter this meditation, play some of your favorite music to get the energy flowing and uplifted in your home. You might like to play some sentimental music that a loved one in the spirit world was fond of. This music will be heard loudly and clearly by your love link in the spirit world.

Now find a comfortable place to sit or lie, and take this extra time to relax. Sit back, and quietly relax, as you take in a few deep breaths, in through your nose and out through your mouth, and again. This meditation of learning, healing, and serenity will help you to understand and cope with the painful experience of losing a loved one. By taking this meditation, you are handing over some of your grief and allowing your guardian angels to help rejuvenate your energy.

Listen to your breath and concentrate on each breath. You will feel yourself drifting off into a sleepy, dozy state, yet fully aware of where you are and your surroundings. You are now feeling yourself drifting into an altered state of your conscious awareness as you start to feel yourself drifting upward. Allow your tears to flow freely, as this is your healing time, and your tears will help to release emotional pain by fertilizing new seeds of growth in life for you.

This meditation is also designed to take you to a higher realm so that you can link with your loved ones in the spirit world, speak with them, and embrace them with the love and light you carry for each other. As you see them and link with them in your meditation, you will be given the inner reassurance that they are free, and happy in the place they now reside, for they are truly in heaven, with our Divine Father, and the energy, love, and light surrounding them in the higher realms is insurmountable. Indeed, your loved ones are now settling into their new role of life in a higher dimension.

Pray for your loved ones each day, sending them love, as they have now transcended from the earth plane and will gain peace from your prayers.

Now, feeling relaxed and settling into your comfortable place, tune out any outside or inside interruptions that may distract you. It is important for you to take this special time out for yourself, a time of understanding and upliftment for you.

Let the Christ white light of love and protection envelop you, so that you can relax and release the emotional pain you have been experiencing, whether it is from the past or present.

Please listen to each word spoken to you; it is best to be guided through this meditation and bought back when the time is right. If you are still playing your favorite music, float with the music, and feel enriched with this time that you have set aside to link with the spirit world. You are feeling so relaxed, protected, and calm as you start on your journey to link with your loved ones. Feeling calm and filled with love, I want you to imagine that you feel as light as a feather, and visualize yourself floating up and up into a gentle breeze. You are as light as a feather, floating upward and upward, feeling such a light soft sensation as you move upward.

As you stop floating, you feel a sense of calm and peace surrounding you, and your heart is not aching at the present moment. In fact, it is filling with joy and happiness as you sense your loved ones around you. Stay in this place of perfection for as long as you like.

You will recognize the change of energy and vibrations entering your room, and you can now feel deep within that your loved ones are experiencing the ultimate gift of peace and love in the spirit world. Your room is filled with the most glorious soft pink light; this is the light of love. Surrounding the edges of your room is the softest color of blue you have ever seen; this is a healing color for you. Your loved one is starting to appear through the haze of pink and blue light. Visualize them in your mind's eye, and you will see a bright white light surrounding them.

We are going to take you on a guided tour to the spiritual realms. This is a tour that you have longed for and justly deserve. As you continue to drift into a deep state of conscious awareness, think about your loved ones in the spirit world, say their name or names in your mind, and call them in. Visualize them, how they were when they were well and happy, living on the earth plane. Again, say their name and speak to them in your mind. Chances are, they will already be settled in, ready to communicate, and awaiting your questions.

To get your attention, your loved ones sometimes will create a familiar smell that you recognize as it drifts past your nose; this may be a favorite flower, fragrance, or perhaps a cooking or tobacco smell. Some people experience the smell of sea air, whichever you experience, just know that this is the time to open up your awareness to the signs that your loved one is giving you of their presence in the room.

Feel your loved one around you, feel the love in the room, speak to them in your mind, and ask them how they are doing. If you feel you are not able to make this connection, then just relax. Our loved ones in the spirit world always make contact with us when the time is right. Do not despair if you feel the link is weak or not being made. Continue talking to your loved one in your mind, as they will hear you loud and clear. It is you, unfortunately, who may not hear them at this time. This may be where you enlist the help of a medium at a later date. Sometimes when our love link is so close, the connection can be very difficult, as our deep emotions can block our communication.

This is a wonderful time for you to recharge your batteries. Do not try too hard to make this connection. You will have meditations in the future, and the connection will come forth. As you take this quiet time, keep sending the love you have in your heart to your loved ones in the spirit world. Visualize them in a place they loved to be when they were on earth and ask them to give you guidance and direction as you get on with your life and enter your new pathway.

See your loved one in the spirit world handing you a rose. What color is your rose? Accept it with love, and tell them that you accept that they are now in the spirit world, that you give them permission to go on in the spirit world, trusting that they will come back and forth to visit you from the spirit world from time to time. Tell them that you accept that they have work to do in the spirit world. As we allow our loved ones to move on, then our lives on the earth plane progress, as they are readily able to make a much better contact with us.

Take your time to heal and deal with your personal pain. It does help to talk about it with those who have the same love vibration and understanding that you have. Take your time and think about your grief and how you can best help others deal with and understand there own.

If you have suffered the loss of a child, then please be consoled to know that they are always met and greeted by a loved one already in the spirit world. It may be a great-grandmother or another loving relative or friend. The spirit world assigns very special "Nursery Mothers" to care and nurture the babies and young ones who come back to the spirit world so quickly.

If you have lost a loved one in an accident, then please know that their spiritual guide would have taken them from their physical bodies only a second before the accident occurred. Their guides would have come from the spirit world to receive them, thus in many cases not allowing them to suffer physical pain.

As you once again visualize your loved one, imagine that they have the brightest gold light surrounding them, as you see them glowing and radiating in this light. Imagine that they are standing near you, and step inside the circle of light surrounding them. Embrace them as you connect in the light, and know that your souls will always be linked in love and light. Stay in your circle of light for as long as you like.

No one can ever remove or take away the deep soul and loving feelings you have for your loved one. These feelings will be embedded in your heart forever. Know that, when you have these deep feelings toward your loved one, when the time is right for you to join them in the spirit world they will come forth to meet you. Only God knows when our time is up in this particular lifetime, and we must let the higher power be the judge of how long we live.

We can change the pattern of almost anything in life, as we all have free will. The only thing we cannot or should not change is how long we live on the earth plane. We must leave this decision to the higher power to decide, the only exception being in cases of terminal illness, where euthanasia is granted.

So take this time of healing and upliftment, knowing that you have an opportunity to connect with your
loved ones in the spiritual world. Feel relaxed and at
peace, happily knowing that your loved ones are near
you, with you, helping you along your spiritual, material, and personal pathway. Stay in this place of peace
and tranquility for a few minutes, before it is time to
come back from your meditation. When you come
back from this time of upliftment, you will feel a
higher energy emerging from within. You will feel so
much brighter and happier within yourself, and your
heart will feel so much lighter. This meditation will
bring you peace of mind, knowing that your loved ones
are embraced with love and light and being cared for in
the spirit world.

On the count of five, come back slowly, bidding
your loved ones farewell. On the count of four, you are
feeling a little sad to say goodbye, but knowing you can
link at almost any time. On the count of three, you are
relaxing and slowly coming back; on the count of two,
slowing move your limbs: On the count of one, slowly
open your eyes and sit for a while until you are ready to
move on. Remember, it helps to share your grief with
your friends and loved ones around you.

To deal with your grief, sit and take these quiet times
of meditation to link with your loved ones. Feel them
within your day-to-day life, and know that they are
always waiting to be reunited with you when the time
is right for you to join them. Spiritual time is like a

blink of an eyelid compared to our time; there is no timing in God's world.

As you awaken from your meditation, hold on to the thought of how important it is for you to be happy, for your happiness will help to brighten the light of your loved ones in the spirit world. Remember your loved ones will watch over you as you continue to link with one another, embracing the spirit of love.

Suggested Reading

Anderson, George and Andrew Barone. *Lessons from the Light: Extraordinary Messages of Comfort and Hope From the Other Side.* New York: G. P. Putnam Sons, 1999.

———. *Walking in the Garden of Souls.* New York: G. P. Putnam Sons, 2001.

Breckenridge, Sandy and Kirk VandenBerghe. *The Seven Sacred Steps: A Practical Guide to Peace and Freedom.* Koloa, Kauai, Hawaii: HeartCore Corp., 2001.

Chopra, Deepak. *Ageless Body, Timeless Mind: The Quantum Alternative to Growing Old.* New York: Three Rivers Press, 1998.

———. *The Path to Love: Spiritual Strategies for Healing.* New York: Three Rivers Press, 1998.

Collins, Judith. *Affirmations for Life.* N.d.

Crawford, Jenny. *Through the Eyes of Spirit.* Nevada City, Calif.: Blue Dolphin Publishing, 1996.

His Holiness, the Dalai Lama. *Ancient Wisdom, Modern World: Ethics for the New Millennium.* London: Abacus, 2001.

Hay, Louise L. *Letters to Louise: The Answers are Within You.* Carlsbad, Calif: Hay House, 1999.

———. *Heal Your Body: The Mental Causes for Physical Illness and the Metaphysical Way to Overcome Them.* Carlsbad, Calif.: Hay House, 1988.

Jordan, Sinda. *Inspired by Angels: Letters from the Archangels.* Nevada City, Calif.: Blue Dolphin Publishing, 1998.

Kübler-Ross, Elisabeth. *On Life After Death.* New York: Simon & Schuster, 1970.

LaGrand, Louis. *Messages and Miracles: Extraordinary Experiences of the Bereaved.* St. Paul: Llewellyn Publications, 1999.

MacLaine, Shirley. *Out on a Limb.* New York: Bantam Doubleday, 1983.

Moore, Kirk. *Tara's Angels: One Family's Extraordinary Journey of Courage and Healing.* Tiburon, Calif.: H. J. Kramer, Starseed Press, 1996.

Newton, Michael. *Journey of Souls: Case Studies of Life Between Lives.* St. Paul: Llewellyn Publications, 1994.

Owens, Elizabeth. *How to Communicate with Spirits.* St. Paul: Llewellyn Publications, 2001.

Stokes, Doris. *A Host of Voices.* London: Futura, 1984.

———. *Voices: . A Doris Stokes Collection.* London: Warner UK, 2000.

———. *Innocent Voices in My Ear.* N.d., 1983

Veary, Nana. *Change We Must.* Medicine Bear Publishing, 1991.

Webster, Richard. *Soul Mates: Understanding Relationships Across Time.* St. Paul: Llewellyn Publications, 2001.

☾ REACH FOR THE MOON

Llewellyn publishes hundreds of books on your favorite subjects! To get these exciting books, including the ones on the following pages, check your local bookstore or order them directly from Llewellyn.

Order by Phone
- Call toll-free within the U.S. and Canada, 1-877-NEW-WRLD
- In Minnesota, call (651) 291-1970
- We accept VISA, MasterCard, and American Express

Order by Mail
- Send the full price of your order (MN residents add 7% sales tax) in U.S. funds, plus postage & handling to:
  Llewellyn Worldwide
  P.O. Box 64383, Dept. 0-7387-0273-0
  St. Paul, MN 55164–0383, U.S.A.

Postage & Handling
- **Standard** (U.S., Mexico, & Canada)
If your order is:
  $20 or under, add $5
  $20.01–$100, add $6
  Over $100, shipping is free
(Continental U.S. orders ship UPS. AK, HI, PR, & P.O. Boxes ship USPS 1st class. Mex. & Can. ship PMB.)
- **Second Day Air** (Continental U.S. only): $10 for one book plus $1 per each additional book
- **Express** (AK, HI, & PR only) [Not available for P.O. Box delivery. For street address delivery only.]: $15 for one book plus $1 per each additional book
- **International Surface Mail:** $20 or under, add $5 plus $1 per item; $20.01 and over, add $6 plus $1 per item
- **International Airmail:** Books—Add the retail price of each item; Non-book items—Add $5 per item

Please allow 4–6 weeks for delivery on all orders.
Postage and handling rates subject to change.

Discounts
We offer a 20% discount to group leaders or agents. You must order a minimum of 5 copies of the same book to get our special quantity price.

Free Catalog
Get a free copy of our color catalog, *New Worlds of Mind and Spirit*. Subscribe for just $10.00 in the United States and Canada ($30.00 overseas, airmail). Call 1-877-NEW-WRLD today!

Visit our website at www.llewellyn.com for more information.

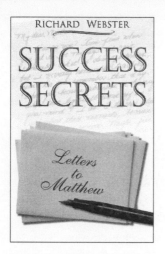

RICHARD WEBSTER

SUCCESS SECRETS

Letters to Matthew

SUCCESS SECRETS
Letters to Matthew
Richard Webster

Matthew is lacking vision and passion in his life. His marriage is on the rocks and his boss is worried about Matthew's falling sales figures. Just as he is feeling the lowest he has felt in years, he goes to his mailbox and finds an envelope addressed to him, with no return address and no stamp. He instantly recognizes the handwriting as that of his old history teacher from high school. Wouldn't Mr. Nevin be dead by now? Why would Matthew get a letter from him after thirty years?

The letter and the others that follow are the backbone of this little book. Each one gives Matthew encouragement and new ways to deal with his life.

After the seventh letter, Matthew sets out to find Mr. Nevin and thank him personally. Mr. Nevin's daughter in-law answers the door, and explains to Matthew that Mr. Nevin passed away five years previously. As the story ends, Matthew ponders the origin of the letters.

This little book is a quick read about following your dreams, setting goals, overcoming obstacles, pushing yourself even further, and making work fun.

1-56718-788-9, 168 pp., 5³⁄₁₆ x 8   **$7.95**

MESSAGES AND MIRACLES
Extraordinary Experiences of the Bereaved

Louis E. LaGrand, Ph.D.

In this moving and compassionate work, one of the pioneers in after-death communication (ADC) research explores the reasons why ADCs occur and how they help the bereaved.

Based on his counseling experience, interviews with numerous people who have had contact with a deceased loved one, and the many questions people have asked him since the the release of his first book, *After Death Communication,* LaGrand unfolds an untapped source of support for the bereaved and those who attempt to comfort them.

Learn whether contact experience is simply the stress of bereavement or an authentic communication, how it can help you establish a new relationship with the deceased, and how to talk to children who report the experience. Read actual accounts of ADCs which have never before appeared in print.

1-56718-406-5, 336 pp., 6 x 9, illus. $12.95

DESTINY OF SOULS
New Case Studies of Life Between Lives
Michael Newton, Ph.D.

A pioneer in uncovering the secrets of life, internationally recognized spiritual hypnotherapist Dr. Michael Newton takes you once again into the heart of the spirit world. His groundbreaking research was first published in the best-selling *Journey of Souls*, the definitive study on the afterlife. Now, in *Destiny of Souls*, the saga continues with seventy case histories of real people who were regressed into their lives between lives. Dr. Newton answers the requests of the thousands of readers of the first book who wanted more details about various aspects of life on the other side. *Destiny of Souls* is also designed for the enjoyment of first-time readers who haven't read *Journey of Souls*.

Hear the stories of people in deep hypnosis as they tell about why we are on earth, the spiritual settings where souls go after death, ways spirits connect with and comfort the living, spirit guides and the council of wise beings who interview us after each life, who is a soulmate and linkages between soul groups and human families, soul recreation and travel between lives, and the soul-brain connection and why we choose certain bodies.

1-56718-499-5, 384 pp., 6 x 9, illus.   **$14.95**

JOURNEY OF SOULS
Case Studies of Life Between Lives
Michael Newton, Ph.D.

This remarkable book uncovers—for the first time—the mystery of life in the spirit world after death on earth. Dr. Michael Newton, a hypnotherapist in private practice, has developed his own hypnosis technique to reach his subjects' hidden memories of the hereafter. The narrative is woven as a progressive travel log around the accounts of twenty-nine people who were placed in a state of super-consciousness. While in deep hypnosis, these subjects describe what has happened to them between their former reincarnations on earth. They reveal graphic details about how it feels to die, who meets us right after death, what the spirit world is really like, where we go and what we do as souls, and why we choose to come back in certain bodies.

After reading *Journey of Souls*, you will acquire a better understanding of the immortality of the human soul. Plus, you will meet day-to-day personal challenges with a greater sense of purpose as you begin to understand the reasons behind events in your own life.

1-56718-485-5, 288 pp., 6 x 9   **$14.95**

HOW TO
COMMUNICATE
WITH SPIRITS

Elizabeth Owens

No where else will you find such a wealth of anecdotes from noted professional mediums residing within a Spiritualist community. These real-life psychics shed light on spirit entities, spirit guides, relatives who are in spirit, and communication with all of those on the spirit side of life.

You will explore the different categories of spirit guidance, and you will hear from the mediums themselves about their first contacts with the spirit world, as well as the various phenomena they have encountered.

In this book, noted mediums residing within a Spiritualist community share their innermost experiences, opinions, and advice regarding spirit communication. It includes instructions for table tipping, automatic writing, and meditating to make contact with spirits.

1-56718-530-4, 240 pp., 5³⁄₁₆ x 8   **$9.95**

SEVEN SECRETS
TO SUCCESS
A Story of Hope
Richard Webster

Originally written as a letter from the author to his suicidal friend, this inspiring little book has been photocopied, passed along from person to person, and even appeared on the internet without the author's permission. Now available in book form, this underground classic offers hope to the weary and motivation for us all to let go of the past and follow our dreams.

It is the story of Kevin, who at the age of twenty-eight is on the verge of suicide after the failure of his business and his marriage. Then he meets Todd Melvin, an elderly gentleman with a mysterious past. As their friendship unfolds, Todd teaches Kevin seven secrets—secrets that can give you the power to turn your life around, begin anew, and reap success beyond your wildest dreams.

1-56718-797-8, 144 pp., 5³⁄₁₆ x 8   **$6.95**

THE LOST SECRETS OF PRAYER
Practices for Self-Awakening
Guy Finley

Do your prayers go unanswered? Or when they are answered, do the results bring you only temporary relief or happiness? If so, you may be surprised to learn that there are actually two kinds of prayer, and the kind that most of us practice is actually the least effective.

Best-selling author Guy Finley presents *The Lost Secrets of Prayer,* a guide to the second kind of prayer. The purpose of true prayer, as revealed in the powerful insights that make up this book, is not to appeal for what you think you want. Rather, it is to bring you to the point where you are no longer blocked from seeing that everything you need is already here. When you begin praying in this new way, you will discover a higher awareness of your present self. Use these age-old yet forgotten practices for self-awakening and your life will never be the same.

Here's what you will discover when you open *The Lost Secrets of Prayer:* seven silent prayers that will turn your life around; the purpose of true prayer; how to touch the timeless truth; the secret power in practicing ceaseless prayer; the best prayer of any kind; how to get more from the universe than you ask for; the real danger of wasted energies; how to develop the unconquerable self in you, and 125 special insights to aid your personal inner work.

1-56718-276-3, 240 pp., 5¼ x 8   **$9.95**

FENG SHUI FOR BEGINNERS
Successful Living by Design
Richard Webster

Not advancing fast enough in your career? Maybe your desk is located in a "negative position." Wish you had a more peaceful family life? Hang a mirror in your dining room and watch what happens. Is money flowing out of your life rather than into it? You may want to look to the construction of your staircase!

For thousands of years, the ancient art of feng shui has helped people harness universal forces and lead lives rich in good health, wealth, and happiness. The basic techniques in *Feng Shui for Beginners* are very simple, and you can put them into place immediately in your home and work environments. Gain peace of mind, a quiet confidence, and turn adversity to your advantage with feng shui remedies.

1-56718-803-6, 240 pp., 5¼ x 8   **$12.95**

MEDITATION FOR BEGINNERS
Techniques for Awareness, Mindfulness & Relaxation
Stephanie Clement, Ph.D.

Perhaps the greatest boundary we set for ourselves is the one between the conscious and less conscious parts of our own minds. We all need a way to gain deeper understanding of what goes on inside our minds when we are awake, asleep, or just not paying attention. Meditation is one way to pay attention long enough to find out.

Meditation for Beginners offers a step-by-step approach to meditation, with exercises that introduce you to the rich possibilities of this age-old spiritual practice. Improve concentration, relax your body quickly and easily, work with your natural healing ability, and enhance performance in sports and other activities. Just a few minutes each day is all that's needed.

Explore many different ways to meditate, including kundalini yoga, walking meditation, dream meditation, tarot meditations, and healing meditations.

0-7387-0203-X, 264 pp., 5⅜₆ x 8, illus.   **$12.95**